The Mass

Dennis C. Smolarski, SJ

LTP

LITURGY
TRAINING
PUBLICATIONS

Acknowledgments

The essays in this book first appeared in issues of the magazine *Liturgy 90,* which was renamed *Rite* in the year 2000, between the years 1991 and 2001. The author, Dennis C. Smolarski, SJ, continues to write the Q&A column in *Rite* magazine. To subscribe go to www.ltp.org or call 1-800-933-4213.

Q&A: THE MASS © 2002 Archdiocese of Chicago: Liturgy Training Publications, 1800 North Hermitage Avenue, Chicago IL 60622-1101; 1-800-933-1800; fax 1-800-933-7094; orders@ltp.org; www.ltp.org. All rights reserved.

Visit our website at www.ltp.org.

This book was edited by David Philippart, with assistance from Gabe Huck and Betsy Anders. Initial design by Anna Manhart, final design by Larry Cope. The production editor was Kris Fankhouser and the typesetting was done by Jim Mellody-Pizzato in Esprit and Officina. Printed by Von Hoffmann Graphics, Inc., of Eldridge, Iowa. The cover and interior art is a modification by Larry Cope of the original Q&A logo designed by Luba Lukova.

Library of Congress Control Number: 2001098354

ISBN 1-56854-358-1

QAMASS

Table of Contents

Introductory Rites

Liturgy of the Word

Liturgy of the Eucharist

Concluding Rites

Ministers

Weekdays

Miscellaneous

Introductory Rites

When there is no music at Mass, how should the entrance and communion antiphons be used?

The *General Instruction of the Roman Missal* (GIRM) is the place to begin looking for the answer. Unlike the *Ritus Servandus* of the Tridentine Missal, the GIRM is fundamentally pastoral in orientation. Since its main concern is the major parish celebration on Sundays and feasts, it does not account for every eventuality, even though it was updated in 2000 in light of pastoral practice since 1969, when the first version appeared.

These factors suggest that one should savor the principles it embodies but always use common sense, especially when applying rubrics intended for sung Sunday celebrations to a weekday liturgy without singing. One should also keep a sense of proper proportion. For example, it is much more important to observe the rubrics regarding consecrating enough bread and wine for everyone in the assembly at each Mass and distributing communion under both kinds whenever possible (2000 GIRM, 85).

Recited entrance and communion antiphons are the least preferred option. The ideal (even at a low-key weekday Mass) is a simple song. After over thirty years of pastoral experience and reflection on the revised *Order of Mass,* it seems that a perfunctory recitation of one verse of scripture encourages a minimalistic approach to liturgy and does not enhance the worship.

The Foreword to the 1975 United States version of the sacramentary offers some practical guidance regarding the entrance and communion verses. Its suggestions (and those contained in the 1975 Appendix to the GIRM) are approved interpretations of the GIRM for the United States. These suggestions are based on a 1970 supplemental Roman document, "On Particular Calendars and Propers," which states that "the point of the entrance antiphon is to direct the thoughts of the congregation to the meaning of the celebration" (#40a). It then says "the text should be such that it can be recited whenever it is not sung and can serve as a basis for the priest's introductory instruction." The Foreword notes that "these brief antiphons are too abrupt for communal recitation." Many are unable to find the correct antiphon and join in the recitation until it is almost finished! Such a situation makes for frustrated worshipers and encourages them not to participate in the future.

The Foreword suggests that "it is preferable to . . . adapt the antiphon and incorporate it into the presentation of the Mass of the day" (that is, after the greeting). The adaptation of the entrance antiphon as part of the introductory comment has been added to the 2000 GIRM at paragraph 48.

The antiphons in the Roman Missal are of two general types: generic and festive. The generic antiphons are generally taken from psalms and are exhortations to worship. The festive antiphons are frequently nonscriptural compositions and are usually related to the festive season or to the saint or feast of the day. Both types provide models of concise remarks to help draw the assembly into the communal actions of praise. In fact, in many places the liturgy might be improved if the presider would limit the introductory comments to a rephrasing of the entrance antiphon and quickly transition to the penitential rite. The following is one example: "My friends, the psalms remind us to praise our God with all of our lives and not put our trust in mere human rulers [Psalm 146]. As we gather to praise our God, let us acknowledge that we have sometimes relied on human strength more than God's grace and let us now ask for forgiveness."

In a similar fashion, a communion antiphon could be integrated into the invitation to communion. (This option is found in the German sacramentary.) Here is an example: "The Lord said: 'I am the bread of life. Those who come to me will never hunger again.' Here is the bread of life—this is the Lamb of God . . . Lord, I am not worthy . . . ."

Again, singing at the entrance and communion times is the best option. If this is not possible, however, a creative integration of the entrance and communion antiphons into the presider's remarks can help focus all present on the great mystery being celebrated.

Which direction should the processional cross face when carried at the head of a procession?

The use of a processional cross appears to date back to at least the fourth century. Prior to the liturgical reforms of the Second Vatican Council, the liturgical books mention its use primarily in conjunction with major outdoor processions such as on Palm Sunday, at funerals or on Corpus Christi. The former Roman Missal does not mention the use of a processional cross at Mass, although historically it seems that a processional cross was placed near the altar after the entrance procession, and this cross was considered the "altar cross" during Mass rather than any cross attached to the wall behind the altar or on the altar itself. (The practice of using the processional cross as the "altar cross" during Mass is still recommended by the 1984 *Ceremonial of Bishops* [CB], 129 and 2000 GIRM, 122.)

From the earliest centuries, the cross has been considered a sign of victory and triumph. Hence, Saint Paul is able to proclaim, "May I never boast of anything except the cross of our Lord Jesus Christ" (Galatians 6:14). It became the honored symbol used to lead Christians in their processions on earth, for it is symbolic of Christ's cross, which guides the life-long pilgrimage of Christians toward heaven. Christians follow Christ as their leader and, symbolically in procession, both Christ and Christians face the same direction as they move from one place to another.

Some of the older rubrical commentaries gave the advice that the "front" of the cross should always be facing the same direction as the person holding the cross. Thus, when a procession is actually in motion, those in the procession would not see the front of the processional cross. This older advice is reiterated in the 1984 *Ceremonial of Bishops.* It states in paragraph 128 that in the entrance procession "an acolyte carrying the cross, with the image to the front" comes after the censer-bearer.

The only times when those involved in a procession would actually see the front of the cross would be when the assembly gathers for an initial rite before the procession begins or for a concluding rite to end a procession. This would occur, for example, when the blessing of palms is done outdoors and the entire assembly is positioned to face the presiding priest and the cross-bearer, who would normally be close to the presider. It would also occur when a funeral procession goes from a church to an adjacent cemetery and the cross-bearer is positioned near the head of the coffin.

The cross is an honored symbol of the core mystery of our faith—that through death comes life. The church is proud to proclaim this mystery to the world. Hence it is only fitting that, when in procession, the "front" of the cross is turned toward the world, into which the Christian community goes to act as a leaven of transformation.

When should the rite of blessing and sprinkling of holy water be used?

The Tridentine rite of sprinkling holy water, the "Asperges," cele-brated before the principal Sunday Mass, was modified in the post-Vatican II revised Roman Missal and integrated into the opening rites of the Mass as an alternative to the penitential rite. The sacramentary notes that it may be celebrated at all Sunday Masses. The *Ceremonial of Bishops* is somewhat stronger, stating that "on Sunday, it is commendable that the rite of blessing and sprinkling water replace the usual penitential rite" (#133). Because this rite is a reminder of baptism, further reflection on its nature offers addi-tional guidelines for its use and celebration.

The most appropriate time for this rite is the Sundays of the Easter Season and Pentecost (2000 GIRM, 51). In contrast, during Lent, as the community prepares with its catechumens for baptism, a standard penitential rite is the better choice. During the rest of the year, the sprinkling of water might regularly be celebrated to emphasize that Sunday is always the "little Easter," the day of bap-tism and new life. Because baptism is entry into the church, the rite is also appropriate at celebrations of the local church such as the anniversary of dedication or patronal feast.

Many communities have yet to experience and understand what a full blessing and sprinkling of baptismal water can mean for an individual and a community. The physical objects we use in this rite are often not up to the task.

For example, metal aspergils (sprinklers) are often so cor-roded that more water stays in the perforated knob than gets sprin-kled on people. As a result, people feel nothing and see nothing coming from such a sprinkler — the action becomes devoid of its intended meaning. "Cemetery sprinklers" that contain water in a plastic shaft can easily become worn, with the knob flying off in a church, crashing into a wall or injuring someone. Some churches regularly use a branch of some plant as a sprinkler, but sometimes the branch is so flexible that even less water gets sprinkled on peo-ple than with a metal sprinkler. I often use a sprinkler common in

Poland. It resembles a small broom: the metal shaft is about twelve inches long, and the straw about ten inches. Sprinkling with this is like sprinkling with a garden hose—there is no doubt that water is being sprinkled.

Small metal water buckets also do not help the assembly experience the fresh water. Some churches use a clear glass bucket or bowl so that the water is visible to the assembly. Such a container may be carried by an assistant.

When the presider alone tries to sprinkle everyone in a large assembly, the opening rites are often disproportionately lengthened. In such situations, it would be better to have water in several containers. After the presider blesses the water, he and others sprinkle different sections of the church. In a smaller group, the entire assembly could process to the bowls of blessed water and sign themselves.

In order to relate the sprinkling rite to baptism even more (if the church architecture allows), it is a good idea to begin the liturgy by blessing the water at the baptismal font itself. During the sprinkling, the ministers could make their way from the font to their seats.

Music for this rite should be well chosen and coordinated with other music during the opening rite. The liturgy presupposes that an appropriate hymn relating to water or baptism will be sung during the sprinkling. The present rubrics also prescribe an opening song and a Gloria. Singing all three in a row usually robs the opening rite of any unity; musicians need to plan carefully. One option is to select a hymn that could be used for the entrance and then continued during the sprinkling rite. Some parishes sing the Gloria during the sprinkling.

Sprinkling with water is a physical rite that can help liturgies achieve a better balance between word and activity. Used regularly on Sundays, it can keep the opening rites oriented toward praise and joy. Planners should always keep in mind, however, that the rite is one of the opening rites. It should never be performed in such a way that it overshadows the celebration of the word and the sharing of the eucharist.

How should the third penitential rite be composed?

The third penitential rite was introduced in the 1969 *Order of Mass* as a contemporary expansion of the Kyrie and an alternative to the communal proclamation of sin, the Confiteor ("I confess . . ."). The invocations of the third penitential rite may be freely improvised, but sometimes newly composed invocations betray fundamental misconceptions about the nature of the Kyrie and the third penitential rite.

One misconception concerns who is being invoked. Years ago it was sometimes stated that the Kyrie invoked all three persons of the Trinity. This interpretation resulted from the heightened Trinitarian emphasis in medieval Western theology. It became commonplace to interpret everything occurring in threes as reflecting the Trinity. An examination of the older tradition, however, indicates that the Kyrie and its liturgical "cousin," the third penitential rite, are in fact addressed to Christ as Lord. The Kyrie is really a shortened form of the cry of the blind men: "Lord, have mercy on us, O Son of David" (Matthew 20:31). Thus any original composition for the invocations of the third penitential rite should be addressed to Christ alone, rather than to Father, Son and Holy Spirit. This has been made explicit in revised sacramentaries of other languages in which the rubrics mention "invocations to Christ."

A second misconception is that the third penitential rite should focus on human sinfulness, even being a kind of examination of conscience. But in the models found in the present English-language sacramentary, the focus is always on Christ, the channel of God's love and mercy. If anything, the officially approved texts form a litany of titles of Jesus such as Prince of Peace, Good Shepherd, Son of Mary, Splendor of the Father and so on. Because the invocations focus on Christ, they should not include the word "we." An invitation such as, "Lord Jesus, for the times we have not seen you present in our neighbors," is the wrong approach. Here the focus is on us, rather than on God's mercy shown in Jesus. Jesus should instead be the subject of the sentence, if you will.

Some have proposed that the third penitential rite should be renamed a "Litany of Praise to Christ." This introductory rite would thus be seen as more appropriate to the joyous seasons of the year rather than as a penitential rite, strictly speaking. This minor adaptation would make the present third penitential rite closer in spirit to the Gloria than to the Confiteor. One can see this already-existing thrust if the paradigms of the sacramentary are carefully examined.

Many people have pointed out how incongruous the public, communal penitential rite often is, especially when sandwiched between a joyous entrance song and a sung Gloria. In a sense, the assembly goes on a roller-coaster ride. For this reason, planners should give careful thought to the choices for the opening rite. On Sundays, especially during the Easter season, the opening rite should employ the blessing and sprinkling of water. During Lent and at special liturgies of penance, one might use the Confiteor or second penitential rite. On festive days and other times of the year, one might choose the third penitential rite and use it as a way to focus the assembly's attention on Christ and to praise the Lord for what he did and continues to do for the church and the world.

Liturgy of the Word

We have been working hard to emphasize the proclamation of the word during Mass. For several years the readers and deacons have been lifting up the lectionary above their heads while saying, "The word [gospel] of the Lord." I recently heard that this practice is now discouraged. Any comments?

Many parishes could enhance their celebration of the liturgy of the word in a variety of ways; one is by showing reverence for the books from which the word is proclaimed. The 1981 *Introduction to the Lectionary* (IL) states the following: "Since, in liturgical celebrations the books, too, serve as signs and symbols of the sacred, care must be taken to ensure that they truly are worthy and beautiful . . . Because of the dignity of the word of God, the books of readings use in the celebration are not to be replaced by other pastoral aids, for example, by leaflets printed for the faithful's preparation of the readings or for their personal meditation" (IL, 35 and 37; see also 2000 GIRM, 349). Clearly, reading from missalettes is out of the question, as is a casual appearance and treatment of the lectionary and the Book of the Gospels. On the other hand, it is possible that an exaggerated reverence for the book may obscure the more important acceptance of the word of God in human hearts. The example of a parallel situation may help clarify this.

For centuries, the Roman church encouraged reverence for the reserved consecrated bread remaining after Mass, yet present legislation insists that this devotion not overshadow the eucharistic action during Mass. The tabernacle is ideally to be in a chapel separated from the main body of the church; benediction immediately after Mass is forbidden; and after the distribution of communion during Mass, the surplus consecrated communion bread is consumed or discreetly placed in the tabernacle. During Mass, what is important is the active participation in the celebration of the eucharist by the assembly and its becoming the body of Christ, rather than worship of the static presence that remains after Mass. St. Augustine emphasize this when he said, "Hear the apostle say . . . 'You are the body of Christ' . . . if you are the body of Christ . . . it is your own symbol which lies on the table, it is your own symbol that you receive."

Similarly, during the liturgy of the word, what is important is that the assembly genuinely hears the word. The proclamation of "The word [gospel] of the Lord" should challenge those present to realize that it is God's word, that "two-edged sword," that was just heard rather than mere human utterances and it should also lead the assembly to allow God's word to take root in their hearts. By holding up the book of scripture during the concluding proclamation, it is possible that the "word of the Lord" may be associated only with the physical book.

The *General Instruction of the Roman Missal* prescribes that appropriate reverence be given to the lectionary, the book of the gospels, and the bread and wine before their use. We are familiar with the solemn procession with the Book of the Gospels from the altar to the ambo (with candles and incense), the procession with the bread and wine from the midst of the assembly to the sanctuary and genuflections after the consecration. But great simplicity characterizes the ritual after the proclamation of the gospel and after communion.

When evaluating a ritual to honor the books of the word, our basic criterion should be this: Appropriate reverence of the books is important because that reverence bespeaks the importance of the living word in the hearts of believers.

Let me suggest some practices that may fit this criterion:

- As the Book of the Gospels is carried in the entrance procession or from the altar to the ambo, the appropriate minister elevates it reverently (2000 GIRM, 120d). This helps focus attention on the dignity of the word and prepares the assembly to listen attentively.

- While proclaiming a reading, the reader or deacon holds the book in his or her hands rather than letting it rest on the ambo. The book is thus seen by the assembly and its reverent handling conveys a sense of its special dignity.

- At the end of the reading, instead of raising the book the reader keeps the book at chest height while looking at the assembly and saying, "The word [gospel] of the Lord." The deacon (or priest) would then lift the book to kiss the gospel text reverently in the sight of all.

Too often the book of God's word has been handled as if it were no more important than a telephone book. The book of God's word is deserving of reverence, so that the words it contains may be reverenced and acted upon by human hearts.

This is the ideal toward which every parish should strive!

What are the pros and cons of using a separate gospel book?

I'll begin by putting this question in a larger context. There are two very impressive processions during the Byzantine eucharistic liturgy. One is the procession with the Book of the Gospels during the liturgy of the word (the "minor entrance"); the other is the procession with the unconsecrated bread and wine during the liturgy of the eucharist (the "great entrance"). In a special way, these "entrances" express Christ's presence in word and sacrament. Christ also is present in the assembly and in the ministers.

Although quite visible in Byzantine liturgies, in the last few hundred years, a Book of the Gospels has been used within Roman liturgies mainly at ordination rites of deacons and bishops. Even at those rites, an altar missal often was substituted. Over the last few years, however, a Book of the Gospels has become a standard feature of Roman liturgy in some places.

Carrying the Book of the Gospels during the entrance procession or during the gospel procession imitates the impressive rite found in the Byzantine liturgy and helps to express and deepen the reverence we give to God's revelation in Christ, as recorded in the gospels. At Mass, the gospel has a designated reader (deacon or priest), a different introduction and conclusion than the other readings and even a special book. Some, however, consider these additions a mixed blessing.

The *General Instruction of the Roman Missal* and the 1981 *Introduction to the Lectionary* both suggest a unity to scripture. All readings are to be proclaimed from the same place, that is, the ambo (2000 GIRM, 309; IL, 33). Although the Book of the Gospels is mentioned in the 2000 GIRM (for example, #120d or #172), it assumes that most often a single lectionary (containing all the readings) will be book used by all those who proclaim the scripture readings (2000 GIRM, 117 and 118b).

The words, objects and actions of the liturgy convey different meanings to different people. The Book of the Gospels can emphasize the respect we give God's word, yet it can also suggest division because it may be used only by an ordained deacon or priest. The Book of the Gospels can highlight the primacy of Christ's words for Christians, yet it can also suggest that other scripture may not be as worthy of our attention.

Should the use of the Book of the Gospels be abandoned? No! Should the Book of the Gospels be used in every church at every Mass? Probably not. *The Introduction to the Lectionary* suggests that the Book of the Gospels is appropriate for cathedrals and larger churches (#36). The Book of the Gospels has an honored place in the liturgical traditions of East and West, yet its use, like the use of incense or other liturgical options, should be determined by balancing various factors. In some parishes, the two major liturgical books (the sacramentary and the lectionary) are carelessly handled. What problems would adding another book raise in these places?

Christ is the reason why Christians gather for prayer, and the revelation of Christ found in the gospels is a key to our understanding and following of him. That much is certain. Using a Book of the Gospels, though important in our liturgical tradition, is always secondary to honoring the person it represents.

The introduction to the *Lectionary for Mass* says that the assembly should keep communal silence after the first and second readings and after the homily. Is this important? If so, what is the best way to introduce this practice?

The *Introduction to the Lectionary* explicitly mentions the role of silence during the proclamation of the word, referring to the *General Instruction of the Roman Missal*. Paragraph 45 of the 2000 GIRM states that "at the conclusion of a reading or the homily, all meditate briefly on what has been heard" (see also 2000 GIRM, 56). The same paragraph concludes: "after communion, they praise and pray to God in their hearts." Since 1970, most parishes have become accustomed to some silence after communion. But for some reason, moments of silence after the readings (during the liturgy of the word) have not become customary, even though the same paragraph of the GIRM mentions both.

Introducing the practice of silence during the liturgy of the word can be done relatively gently in one of two ways.

Since the IL also suggests silence "before this liturgy begins" (#28) after all are seated at the conclusion of the opening prayer, the reader slowly walks toward the ambo. Only when the assembly has settled into an attentive silence does the reader begin the first reading.

At the end of the reading, the reader could pause for fifteen to thirty seconds before announcing "The word of the Lord," and then slowly walk away. After the reader is seated, the psalmist stands to begin the psalm. A similar procedure can be followed by the second reader and the deacon who proclaims the gospel.

This would necessitate that all readers, including the gospel reader, rehearse how long a pause is long enough, since the tendency will be to rush. Moreover, this approach requires that the assembly be catechized (perhaps by way of the bulletin or brief announcements made before liturgy begins) so that people aren't distracted by thinking that the reader has forgotten the last line. Of course, this approach also presumes that the reader is able to bring the reading to a successful conclusion and avoid the impression that he or she simply stopped reading.

Another approach would be to train the psalmist and the musicians to gauge the silence. The reader proclaims the scripture and concludes immediately with "The word of the Lord." Then the reader sits. The psalmist and the musicians wait a minute or so before beginning the psalm or the gospel acclamation. Once again, the assembly needs to be catechized so as not to be distracted by thinking that someone doesn't know what to do. And, as already mentioned, rehearsal is necessary so that the psalmist and the musicians know how long is long enough to pause. The tendency during the liturgy, when the assembly is present and some are shifting in their seats or clearing their throats, will be to rush.

After the homily, the presider can return to the chair (if he did not give the homily from the chair), sit for a moment and then stand and begin the creed. When the assembly begins to get comfortable with these new moments of reverential silence, they can be lengthened as appropriate. The habit of keeping communal silence will slowly grow stronger if it is worked at diligently.

Perhaps more than the liturgy of the eucharist, the liturgy of the word can become overly verbose—words, words and more words. In most parishes, the only texts sung are the psalm and the gospel acclamation. In such a situation, silence is not an "extra" that can be easily omitted, but is something necessary to savor and digest God's word. As paragraph 56 of the 2000 GIRM says, "any sort of haste that hinders recollection must be clearly avoided (see also IL, 28)." Our culture is frenetic enough without God's people being subjected to haste while it tries to hear the holy word addressed to it during liturgy. There is a significant danger that the one word may get lost among the many words.

One of our priests and some of our lectors want the readers to go to the presider to receive a blessing before doing the first or second reading. Is this a good idea?

In comparison with other liturgical families, the Roman liturgical tradition has shown a certain restraint and in some cases even a bit of austerity in its rituals. That sort of simplicity in details can help the assembly focus on what is truly important and not get distracted with secondary details.

Although it is not prescribed by the rubrics, among some users of the Byzantine rite (for example, the Russians) the reader approaches the presiding priest during the singing of the Trisagion and receives a blessing before proclaiming the first reading. But this practice is quite private and similar to the non-prescribed blessings often given to servers before they vest.

In describing the liturgy of the word, the various Roman liturgical books direct the reader to go to the ambo, read the reading with skill and reverence and then return to his or her place (see 2000 GIRM, 128 and 196; IL, 55; CB, 32). The only gesture that the reader does is a profound bow when passing in front of the altar (see 2000 GIRM, 275; CB, 72). By not prescribing any other action or prayer, the Roman rite invites the assembly to focus on the reading itself rather than on the reader. In a sense, the solemn blessing of readers and eucharistic ministers when they are formally instituted in their ministry is a blessing that prepares them for their ministry at every liturgy in which they carry our their duties; thus, additional blessings are not needed.

One might object, however, on the basis that because a deacon gets a special blessing at each Mass before proclaiming the gospel, similar blessings should be given to other readers as well—and such an argument is not without a certain logic!

In response to such an argument, though, one should note that the blessing of the deacon (or the prayer of the priest if there is no deacon) is part of a special complex of ritual words and gestures that distinguish the gospel as the high point of the liturgy of the word. Not only is the gospel reader given a special blessing, but other ritual elements also are included that are not prescribed for the other readings such as candles, a special book, incense, a preparatory acclamation and the posture of standing. As only one part of a series of ritual elements, the blessing of the deacon does not usually call attention to itself, particularly if it's done discreetly (as the rubrics prescribe) while the Alleluia is sung by the assembly.

In contrast, the readings that precede the gospel are proclaimed with much more restraint. The assembly remains seated, there are no preliminary acclamations and incense and candles are not used. This is a time to focus on re-hearing our story as a people of faith, a story that culminates in the proclamation of the gospel and the words of Christ.

In addressing liturgical renewal, the *Constitution on the Sacred Liturgy* cautions us about introducing changes into the liturgy based on personal initiative (#22.3). Although this warning is sometimes cited when prohibiting omissions or textual changes, the conciliar decree also explicitly forbids arbitrarily adding elements to the liturgy. I would suggest that this is particularly true regarding additions that may distort the stark simplicity of focus that is part of the genius of the Roman rite.

To summarize, it seems to me that the blessing of readers is a practice that has the potential to distract the assembly from its primary focus, which is the proclaimed word. It would be better if it were not introduced into contemporary liturgical practice.

From where should the cantor lead the responsorial psalm—from the music stand or the ambo? Should the cantor be vested? If so, in what—an alb or a choir robe?

The 1981 *Introduction to the Lectionary* states that after the first reading the "psalmist," that is, the cantor of the psalm, leads the psalm at the ambo (#22). This direction echoes what is found in the 2000 *General Instruction of the Roman Missal,* which adds the provision that the psalmist may proclaim the psalm from some "other suitable place" (#61). (See also 2000 GIRM, 309.)

The ambo is the place from which the word of God is proclaimed. Historically, the ambo was an elevated platform with a reading desk. After the first reading from the ambo's steps, the psalm was sung by a psalmist. (Because the Latin word for the ambo's steps was *gradus,* the psalm sung after the first reading became known as the gradual.) This psalm is more than a meditation hymn or musical interlude between proclamations of God's word. It is itself the sacred word, given to us to be sung back to the Lord (IL, 19). That is why communities that substitute hymns for the psalm or for similar scriptural canticles are stepping outside of the tradition and going beyond the norms of permitted substitutions.

Because the psalm is part of the word of God that the liturgy proclaims, it is appropriate that the person leading it do so from the ambo, the same place at which the other readings are proclaimed. This is why both 2000 GIRM (#309) and IL (#33) mention that the ambo is reserved for the readings and the responsorial psalm, and that announcements should be given and all other music should be led from another lectern. (See also 2000 GIRM, 105b.)

One of the most prayerful proclamations of the psalm that I have ever experienced was in an African American parish. At that Mass, the psalmist, who was a member of the vested gospel choir but was not the cantor for the rest of the liturgy, went to the ambo and led the psalm, sung in a contemporary "psalm tone."

The assembly participated full-voiced in the response. The psalm was truly proclaimed as part of the liturgy of the word, and the assembly sang God's praise by singing the very words of scripture.

Most parishes, however, do not have a psalmist apart from the cantor, and so the psalm is often led by the cantor. In this situation, assuming that the cantor exercises his or her ministry from some place other than the ambo, it may be appropriate for him or her to lead the psalm from there instead of going to the ambo. This certainly is preferable to the reader merely reciting the psalm at the ambo. But having the cantor sing the psalm at the music stand gives the impression that the psalm is just one more hymn to be sung. It does not emphasize its unique character as scripture that is part of the proclamation of God's word. The psalm is not a processional hymn or a hymn to cover an action (such as the Lamb of God), but it is sung scripture proclaimed for its own sake. That may be reason enough for the cantor to make the journey to the ambo.

Those liturgies at which readers or choir members are vested, it would certainly be appropriate for a psalmist to be vested similarly. Consistency in vesture among ministers is important: Subtle, unintended messages can be conveyed if the psalmist is vested and the readers are not, and vice-versa. The white alb is the vesture proper to all the baptized, yet there is nothing wrong with the psalmist wearing the choir robe if he or she also sings in the choir.

What is important in determining or modifying local practice is that the psalm be experienced as an integral part of the liturgy of the word, as well as the assembly's way of responding to God's word by singing God's word. The location from which the psalm is led and the vesture of the one leading it can both assist in realizing this experience, and thus they should not be overlooked. Yet the final determination of local custom should be the nature of the local assembly. Communities should never cease trying to improve their liturgy and reflect authentic tradition, but antiquarianism is not an end in itself.

When should we use a "seasonal" psalm after the first reading on Sunday rather than the one assigned in the lectionary? The parish musicians sometimes choose an alternative that is easily sung but has little to do with the readings, whereas the appointed psalm and its refrain often give an appropriate insight into the gospel's core message.

The norms concerning substituting another psalm for the psalm assigned for the day by the lectionary are found at paragraph 89 of the 1981 *Introduction to the Lectionary,* as well as in the rubric before paragraph 173 in the revised lectionary (or before paragraph 174 in the old lectionary). (See also 2000 GIRM, 61.) The presupposition in all places is that a substitution is permitted only if the psalm will be sung.

All these norms are generous in allowing a substitution "that the people may be able to join in the psalm response more readily." In fact, the lectionary itself gives two alternatives: (1) alternative refrains that may be used with the psalm of the day (paragraph 173; paragraph 174 in the old lectionary) and (2) alternative psalms (paragraph 174; paragraph 175 in the old lectionary). In both cases, the alternatives are grouped by liturgical season, ensuring that the alternative refrains or psalms are still in some way appropriate to the readings.

In addition to the alternative psalms found in the lectionary, the GIRM permits the use of alternative psalms found in the *Simple Gradual,* published in 1967. But it is rare that people have access to this collection of texts.

When the English translation of the 1969 *Order of Mass* was approved, the U.S. bishops also approved an extension of the provisions of paragraph 36 of the 1969 GIRM (2000 GIRM, 61) for the psalm and this extension was renewed in 2001. (All the extensions are found in the U.S. Appendix to GIRM, at the front of the sacramentary.) The U.S. extension allows other psalms, in addition to those given in the lectionary and the simple gradual, as long as they are chosen in harmony with the season or the feast. But texts that are not psalms (or "psalm-like," such as the scriptural canticles) are not permitted.

Which psalm to use should be a pastoral decision based on which option would be most beneficial for the community. (See 2000 GIRM, 360–61.) By its very nature, a psalm is meant to be sung. Perhaps some communities may find it difficult to sing a new refrain melody each week, or that it is difficult for the cantor to learn to sing a new psalm text each week. In such cases, an alternative seasonal refrain or seasonal psalm—one that would be used for several weeks—would be appropriate. In other communities, it might not be a burden for the assembly to sing a new refrain every week, as long as these refrains are well chosen or easy to sing. In these communities, if using the psalm of the day is possible given the resources and abilities of the community, then the psalm of the day is preferable because it probably contains sentiments echoing themes in the first reading or gospel.

Unfortunately, some parish musicians too quickly dismiss (or do not even consider) the psalm given in the lectionary but attempt to substitute a "meditation" song, which may not even be a psalm or be scripturally-based. The literary genre of a psalm is special. It is a hymn of the community to God or in praise of God and serves a special purpose in the liturgy of the word. The assembly, using the word of God, responds in song to the word of God just proclaimed. Thus every effort should be made to sing the response and use an appropriate psalm as that response.

There is something to be said about using melodies that are familiar to an assembly. Such a practice enables those present to sing with confidence. Thus it is usually good to use one setting of the Sanctus, Memorial Acclamation and Amen for several weeks or for one liturgical season rather than using a different setting each week. A similar approach could apply to the psalm if a seasonal refrain is used by the assembly, while the cantor sings the psalm of the day. This approach has the benefit of using the psalm of the day as well as enabling the assembly to use a familiar response. Unfortunately, in my experience, this option is rarely tried.

Even after more than thirty years of using the current order of Mass, we are still striving to understand its implications and realize its options. We may also still need occasional catechesis, lest we misinterpret various elements of the rite.

The liturgical ideal is to have the responsorial psalm sung enthusiastically by the entire assembly in response to the proclamation of the first reading. Ideally, the psalm used is the psalm of the day. But if circumstances suggest that another psalm be substituted, then this is permitted in order to engage the assembly in song as they praise the wonders God has done for us.

What's the story behind the sequences that appear between the second reading and the gospel acclamation on Easter Sunday and Pentecost? Should they be sung? If so, how can we encourage the assembly to do so?

In the 1570 missal of Pius V, there were several feasts and occasions for which the texts for the Mass included a poetic hymn called the "sequence" to be sung or recited before the proclamation of the gospel. One of the more famous of these hymns was the *Dies Irae* ("Day of Wrath") of the funeral Mass. The rubrics of the Tridentine missal prescribed that the sequence was to be sung after the gradual and Alleluia (and its verse) but before the repetition of the Alleluia. In origin, it seems to have been an elongation of the sentiments of the Alleluia verse, but in function it played the role of an elongated meditation after the gradual. This role of the sequence as a meditation hymn was fostered by the practice that saw the Alleluia as a conclusion to the gradual (and therefore a meditation hymn to be listened to while seated) rather than as a preparation for the gospel (and therefore to be sung by all while standing).

The present sacramentary and lectionary retain only two "obligatory" sequences—those for Easter Sunday and Pentecost. The sequences for the solemnity of the Body and Blood of Christ *(Lauda, Sion)* and for Our Lady of Sorrow *(Stabat Mater)* have been retained among the available texts for optional use.

The 1969 *General Instruction of the Roman Missal* was rather laconic in its instructions about the sequence. Because it is an element of the liturgy inserted before the gospel only on rare occasions, the reference to the sequence occurs in what may seem to be an afterthought sentence (#40), which states the following: "Sequences are optional, except on Easter Sunday and Pentecost."

We get more insight into the sequence's function in the instructions for the *Ordo Cantus Missae* (OCM), which was published in 1972, three years after the GIRM. In contrast to the practice of the Tridentine missal, in paragraph 8 the rubrics specifically mention that the sequence is supposed to be sung after the final Alleluia of the acclamation before the gospel, and this is where the latest editions of books of Gregorian chant place the sequence. (Unfortunately, the translation of this document that appears in *Documents of the Liturgy* [DOL] omits the phrase "after the last Alleluia" in paragraph 4287.) The 2000 GIRM has been updated to avoid any ambiguity and now reads thus: "The sequence is sung after the Alleluia. It is optional, except on Easter Sunday and Pentecost" (#64).

According to the OCM, in the present *Order of Mass* the Alleluia (with its verse) is seen as a welcome of the gospel rather than as a concluding meditation to the previous reading (as in the Tridentine Mass). Coming after the Alleluia and its verse, the sequence now plays the role of an elongated pre-gospel welcoming hymn, highlighting the proclamation of the gospel on a special occasion.

Of course, it is always easier to sing a hymn according to a known melody than to one that is unknown. Although the Pentecost sequence ("Come, O Holy Spirit, come") was often used in other contexts (for example, as a hymn during confirmations), the Easter sequence was less successful as a well-known congregational hymn. As a result, if the Easter sequence was not omitted it seemed to be an intrusion into the flow of the liturgy by being recited by the entire assembly or sung by a soloist.

Some recently published hymnals and missalettes offer alternative metrical translations of the sequences (particularly the Easter sequence) that can be sung to a familiar melody. Some well-known hymns are also partial paraphrases of various sequences (such as "Christ the Lord is ris'n today") and are sometimes suggested as alternatives for congregational use.

There are two major problems with our use or non-use of the sequence. The first problem is that the sequence is often reduced to a long text that is merely recited. The final sentence of paragraph 8 of the OCM, however, flatly states the following: "When the Alleluia and its verse are not sung, the sequence is omitted." This norm highlights that both the Alleluia and the sequence are meant to be joy-filled, sung acclamations rather than texts to be recited.

The other problem concerns when the sequence is sung in relation to the Alleluia. The initial editions of the Latin lectionary placed the sequence before the Alleluia, and this is the position in which it appears in most English lectionaries. But this is not the position in which the sequences appear in the revised Latin books of chants, published after the Latin lectionary, nor is it the position specified in the 2000 GIRM. If sung before the Alleluia, the sequence loses its original function as an elongation of the sentiments of the Alleluia and is turned into a meditation. When sung after the Alleluia, it can serve as a processional hymn for an elaborate gospel procession on two of the most important days of the church year.

It is a standard liturgical principle that we highlight special days in special ways. On the first and last days of the paschal season, the church has retained hymns to be sung as a way to welcome the gospel during Mass. Our challenge is to use this liturgical heritage in creative ways to enhance the proclamation of Christ's good news.

Is it a good practice to proclaim the gospel in parts at other times of the year, as is done on Passion Sunday and Good Friday?

The sacramentary specifically permits the proclamation of the passion by several readers—traditionally three deacons—on Passion (Palm) Sunday and on Good Friday. This form of proclamation is also referred to in the *Directory for Masses with Children,* where it specifically mentions that "where the text of the readings suggest," this form of proclamation "may be helpful" in Masses with children (#47).

Thus, although the sacramentary does not explicitly permit the practice apart from the proclamation of the passion during Holy Week, it would seem that by the authority of the *Directory for Masses with Children,* one can justify proclaiming any of the readings in parts, when children are present and the texts lend themselves to such a proclamation.

However, just because such a format for proclaiming the readings may be possible, it does not always mean that its use is helpful! (See 2000 GIRM, 109.)

The solemn proclamation of the passion in parts dates to the Middle Ages when popular piety, combined with an official liturgy that few could understand, led to the introduction of various dramatic practices into the devotional life of Christians. Passion plays, stations of the cross, nativity scenes and lifelike crucifixes all became popular during a time when authentic eucharistic devotion was deficient. One way of describing this is to say that "memory" was replaced by "mimicry." Instead of remembering what Christ did, and seeing his life as giving us hope in our contemporary struggles, people settled for a dramatic reenactment of the events of his life.

For example, it was in this era that people wanted to have donkeys on Palm Sunday. Because they did not see their own life-journeys reflected in the tension between palms and passion, they needed to liven up the unintelligible liturgy with dramatic touches that solely commemorated what happened in Jerusalem. Their piety focused on venerating plaster corpuses on lifelike crucifixes on Good Friday rather than honoring the barren "wood of the cross." They created tombs and life-size images so they could honor Christ in his grave on Holy Saturday.

The same tendency to replace "memory" with "mimicry" is still evident when priests break the host during the institution narrative of the eucharistic prayer, when the Holy Thursday gospel is interrupted to include the footwashing, or when gospel passages are acted out or even mimed rather than proclaimed.

In authentic liturgy, the sacred story in scripture is proclaimed so that our memory can give us strength to live in the present with our faces set toward the future. Drama often leaves us with mere mimicry and nostalgic sentimentality for a bygone past. Because these emotions cannot be rationally explained away, but through symbol affect us unconsciously, we must be cautious, lest inappropriate options used at liturgies reinforce tendencies that are ultimately detrimental to good liturgy.

In general, then, I would be very cautious about proclaiming any scripture passage in parts except in very special situations, such as at a Mass for small children, where it actually helps their comprehension in understanding the present-day implications of the biblical narrative. Alternatively, it might sometimes be helpful to have a succession of readers reading a longer passage rather than having several readers attempt a dramatic reenactment. The uniqueness and the starkness of the rites of Good Friday may help keep the memory aspect (and dignity) of John's passion prominent, but otherwise I would suggest that less dramatic options may lead to a better overall experience of scripture in the liturgy.

Is it permissible or appropriate for a priest or deacon to preach at all the parish Masses, but only participate in one full Mass?

My childhood memories include Latin Masses, at which one priest would say the Mass and another, the Sunday preacher, would deliver the sermon and help distribute communion. Aside from the sermon and communion, the second priest was absent from the sanctuary. This disconnection between the preacher and the Mass was tolerated by the *Ritus Servandus* of the Tridentine Missal, which speaks about the "preacher" as if here were assumed to be someone other than one of the ministers of the Mass.

Reestablishing the classical tradition, the *2000 General Instruction of the Roman Missal* states that "the homily should ordinarily be given by the priest celebrant" (#66). The GIRM does state that the deacon "at times preaches God's word" (#94), and at concelebrations, "one of the concelebrants" may give the homily (#213). However, as a general rule, "it . . . belongs to the priest presiding to proclaim the word of God" (#31). This principle is also found in the 1981 *Introduction to the Lectionary,* especially in paragraph 41: "The one presiding exercises his proper office and the ministry of the word of God also as he preaches the homily." (See also #24 and 38.) The *Directory for Masses with Children* makes provision for one of the adults present at Masses with children to speak to them after the gospel if the priest finds preaching to children difficult (#24).

Certainly, it seems to be against the spirit of the renewed liturgy to allow individuals who do not participate in the entire liturgy to exercise a key liturgical role in that same liturgy. The GIRM assumes that when someone other than the presiding priest preaches the homily, that person is present for the entire liturgy and participates fully. (See #66.)

The vision given by the GIRM and the *Introduction to the Lectionary* is that part of the office of presiding at the eucharist is to proclaim God's word through preaching the homily, similar to the duty of proclaiming thanksgiving through praying the eucharistic prayer. The homily is presented as an integral part of the order of worship and an integral part of the presiding priest's office (2000 GIRM, 65–66). It is therefore inappropriate that, as a regular practice, someone other than the presider preach during Mass. However, there may be reasons why, on occasion, a nonpresiding preacher may be fitting. For example, a married deacon may be able to speak about family life with more credibility than a celibate priest. At Masses with a large number of children, another adult may preach. At funerals, it may be appropriate for one priest friend of the deceased to preside while another concelebrates and preaches the homily.

What about special appeals? It is not uncommon for missionaries to be invited to speak to raise funds for their apostolates. Yet such "appeals" are frequently inappropriate as homilies based on the readings or liturgy of the day. In situations where such a visitor is not the presiding priest (or a concelebrant) at a Mass, it might be more appropriate for a short appeal to be given after the prayer after communion and before the final blessing. In such cases, the presiding priest would preach the homily, perhaps appropriately shortened for the occasion. Even if the visitor presides or concelebrates, the homily should be more than an appeal for money for a specific cause. The homily is always to be based on the readings or liturgy of the day and be appropriate to the local assembly. Being a missionary does not exempt one from following the norms of good parish liturgy! Perhaps parish staffs could correspond with the visitor before his or her arrival and clarify in what context the person will speak and what is expected.

What about pastoral burnout and the inability of some priests to deliver a top-quality homily week after week? Preparing and delivering liturgical homilies is part of an ordained minister's office. This task, like other aspects of ministry, takes time and energy, and the results may be better some weeks than others. It is easy to appeal to various reasons to justify retaining some version of the pre-Vatican II practice. Such a practice, however, compromises basic liturgical and ecclesial principles. It is part of the "job description" of the presiding priest to preach the homily, and it is part of ritual authenticity that liturgical ministers be present throughout the liturgy. Even after thirty years, we are still uncomfortable with the radical demands that the renewed liturgy sometimes makes of us.

The homily is a significant moment in the eucharistic celebration. It must be of good quality; it must also be experienced as an integral part of the entire celebration. Our revised liturgical books present us with a vision of how this integration should take place. This vision is the ideal toward which every parish should strive!

What are the regulations for writing the general intercessions? What form should the petitions take?

It is difficult to speak of "regulations" for the form of the general intercessions because the 2000 *General Instruction of the Roman Missal* does not address this issue directly (see #69–71). Hence, to understand the common literary form, we must look to the technical meanings of the specific words used and to the examples found in the sacramentary.

When referring to what are often called the "petitions," the GIRM uses the word "intentions" (#70, 71, 177 and 197). An "intention" is a topic or focal point for prayer, and this word is also commonly used when requesting that a Mass be offered for a specific "intention." In itself, an "intention" is not a petition, intercession or prayer, but the focal point for subsequent prayer. It is a simple statement by one person to another. Thus the topics for prayer that are announced as part of the general intercessions are to be worded as "intentions" to be announced, not prayers to be offered.

There are two places in the sacramentary where sample texts can be found and used as models for the general intercessions. One, the liturgy of Good Friday, has texts dating back several centuries. The other, Appendix I, contains texts composed when the Roman Missal was revised in the late 1960s.

The older Good Friday intercessions are of a special and ancient Roman style in which a particular prayer follows each intention and, traditionally, the audible response of the assembly is limited to a simple "Amen" to conclude the presider's prayers. Nevertheless, the literary style of the "intention" is noteworthy in that each one is obviously a statement directed to the assembly rather than a prayer to God (the first and last even beginning with the words "Dear friends"). The revised rubrics of the sacramentary (based on the rubrics in the *Ceremonial of Bishops*) explicitly state that these introductory intentions are to be announced by the deacon rather than by the presiding priest (as had been the custom in the Tridentine Missal).

This literary form of the intention, that is, a text addressing the assembly, is the form retained for the intercessions found in the sample texts in the Appendix of the sacramentary. In all cases, the deacon (or another minister other than the presider) is speaking to the assembly and announcing to them what they should pray for. Each of these texts could be prefaced with the following words: "My dear brothers and sisters." In this way, the logic of the text would continue to make sense. The real "prayer of the faithful" occurs when the assembly prays silently or gives voice through a common response such as "Lord, hear our prayer," "Kyrie, eleison" or similar texts addressed to Christ or God the Father.

The Roman tradition is that a deacon or other minister does not say any "prayer," that is, a text addressed to God. Such texts are reserved to the presider, who offers them in the name of the entire assembly. In a few cases, the assembly as a whole may pray to Christ (as in the memorial acclamation) or sing a hymn to God (as in the Gloria). But our liturgical tradition gives to the presiding priest the role of praying to God in the name of the entire assembly.

The basic structure of the general intercessions, according to paragraph 71 of the GIRM, is as follows: The presider (and not a concelebrant or other minister) introduces the general intercessions by speaking to the assembly and inviting them to pray for the needs of the church and the world. The deacon, cantor or another minister announces the "intentions," which are worded so that he or she is addressing the assembly. Each "intention" usually concludes with the same words so that the assembly knows when to offer their common response. This common response is the prayer. After the last intention and response, the presider (and not a concelebrant or other minister) prays a collect-style prayer that sums up the prayers of the assembly and concludes the intercessions.

By tradition, the intercessions are in the style of a litany, and litanies are intended to be sung. Thus it is most appropriate that the intentions be sung. If this is not possible, an alternative is for the cantor to sing the concluding invitation and response even if a deacon or other minister recites the intentions. In such a situation, it would be permitted to adapt the text of the concluding invitation to match the text of the response. In other words, when the invitation is sung to elicit a response by the assembly, it may be worded as a prayer to Christ in the fashion of an intonation. For example, the cantor might sing, "Lord, in your mercy," and the assembly would conclude, "Hear our prayer." In this case, the entire phrase, "Lord, in your mercy, hear our prayer," should be considered a single response to the intention, sung in two parts: the first half by the cantor and the second half by the entire assembly. (This invitation and response is commonly used in Great Britain.)

The intercessions found in the Liturgy of the Hours are in a different format. This was purposely done when the Liturgy of the Hours was revised to make the intentions of the intercessions suitable when celebrating Morning or Evening Prayer alone. These intentions are always directed to Christ or God the Father and, in a sense, take the form of a modern antiphonal psalm. By this I mean that, as the psalms are prayer texts directed to God and often prayed alternatingly, so the intentions of these intercessions are arranged so that the first half of each intention is proclaimed by a reader and the second half is proclaimed by the assembly. Only when this antiphonal format is not possible (as when the assembly does not have the text) does the assembly offer a simple repeated response.

Some liturgical books have unfortunately (in my mind) included both these different forms of intercessions when printing alternatives together, such as in the *Order of Christian Funerals*. In paragraph 167 of the U.S. edition, there are two different sample general intercessions for use during a funeral Mass, but the first option is of the style found in Morning or Evening Prayer (each intention is addressed to Christ), while the second option is the classical form for use during Mass.

One should note that the revised funeral rite was promulgated in 1969, before the revised Missal was published, and that in the original edition, the sample texts for the general intercessions were included only in an appendix, with a small rubric, "For use at Mass or at a liturgy of the word." I recommend that the "direct prayer" style of intercession found in the Liturgy of the Hours not be used during Mass but only in other types of services.

Finally, there is a growing tendency to turn each intention into a somewhat lengthy mini-homily with a convoluted grammatical structure. Rather than inspiring prayer by the assembly, such texts often confuse those who hear them. What our assemblies need are intentions that are direct and succinct (see 2000 GIRM, 71), and which remind the assembly of concerns for prayer and of actions that can aid our brothers and sisters in need.

Can members of the assembly offer spontaneous intercessions during the general intercessions at Mass? And how rigid is the order of the topics of the intercessions?

Ever since the reintroduction of the general intercessions in the Roman Mass, there have been various ways of understanding this part of the liturgy, ways that have led to a multiplicity of practices and customs. The alternative title for the general intercessions, "prayers of the faithful," highlights the active involvement of the assembly in this part of the liturgical action. But the classical form of the intercessions, the form of a litany, suggests that the active involvement of the assembly in prayer is limited to a response (ideally sung) after each of the intentions, which are traditionally announced by a deacon.

Focusing on the intercessions as "prayers of the faithful" has prompted some people to word the intentions as prayers rather than as statements to the assembly (contrary to the examples found in the sacramentary), to have multiple ministers announce the intentions or even to permit anyone present to announce a prayer intention. Since the *General Instruction of the Roman Missal* gives very few guidelines regarding the general intercessions, this part of the liturgy admits of some variety. But one should, at the same time, respect its nature and its traditional form. (See 2000 GIRM, 69–71; IL, 30–31.)

Perhaps one of the most moving executions of the general intercessions that I have seen was at a Mass celebrated by Pope John Paul II at the Mall in Washington, D.C. Each intention was announced by a different person in a different language, representing the diversity of ancestries that our country comprises. Yet each intention was concluded by the same sung invitation to prayer, and the same response was sung by all the faithful gathered at the liturgy.

A document on Masses with special groups, issued in May 1969 (*Actio pastoralis* [DOL, 2120 ff.]), addresses the participation by those present in the general intercessions. This document states that when the assembly is small and homogeneous, it is permissible for those present to participate by adding "some particular intention." One cautionary note expressed is that the intentions should be "properly prepared ahead of time." Another caution mentioned is that care be taken to avoid the "complete omission of the general intentions." This document expresses the concern that something as formal as praying for the needs of the church and the world should not be completely left up to haphazard spontaneity.

Paragraph 70 of the 2000 GIRM suggests the typical order of the intentions: first for the church, then for world needs and national concerns, then for those in special need and finally for the particular concerns of the local community. Although four topics are mentioned, the GIRM never explicitly limits the number of intentions to four but only suggests that the order generally follow the pattern it gives, a traditional pattern found in intercessory litanies.

One drawback to inviting everyone in the assembly to participate in the general intercessions in larger groups (presuming that everyone can hear each petition) is that an imbalance occurs in the focus of the intercessory prayer. Ideally, the intercessions are the moment when the local community consciously transcends its own needs and problems and exercises a ministry for the wider community, that is, for the universal church and the world as a whole. In some places, spontaneous intentions offered by the assembly at weekday liturgies have become customary, and those present have learned to focus their concerns on the wider society. But in other places, such spontaneous intentions can be experienced as a low point of the liturgy, particularly if they are rambling or repetitious. Quite often, such spontaneous prayers are a sequence of repeated announcements of "For a special intention, let us pray to the Lord." Such "special intentions" that are unnamed and unspecified can be jarring in a prayer form that should regularly serve to make those present aware of the specific needs of society.

When the number of spontaneous intentions is disproportionately large and the focus of such intentions is narrowly restricted to individual and personal concerns, the nature of the general intercessions is altered. It is no longer an exercise of the priestly duty of the baptized in interceding for others (2000 GIRM, 69). Instead, it has become an exercise in self-examination in which the wider community and the world can seem to be afterthoughts.

As with any part of the liturgy, the manner of celebrating the general intercessions at Mass should occasionally be a topic of reflection and examination by those charged with overseeing the community's liturgy. There are many ways to encourage active involvement in the intercessions without shifting their focus or form. And no one way will work equally well in all settings. One method is to have the assembly sing their response, which can work well with larger groups, for example, at Sunday Masses. At other Masses, such as at larger weekday liturgies, a deliberate period of silence after each response can be very beneficial. In Masses for smaller groups, including smaller weekday Masses, participation by members of the assembly in announcing the prayer intentions can be a grace-filled time, especially when the assembly comes to know the faith of its members as individuals who pray for those in need, both in the local community and in the wider community that makes up our church and world.

When is the best time or dismissing catechumens after the homily at Sunday Mass—before or after the general intercessions?

Parishes that take seriously the responsibility to initiate adults often solemnly dismiss the catechumens whenever they are present at Mass. Although people may be familiar with the dismissal of catechumens at the rite of acceptance into the order of catechumens and at the scrutinies during Lent, following the counsel given in the RCIA (#83.2 in the U.S. edition), such dismissals are appropriate whenever catechumens are present at Mass and are able to remain together for further prayer and catechesis.

Most agree that it is an anomaly for those who are not baptized (and thus cannot receive the eucharist) to be present for the eucharistic action. Since the RCIA has also reintroduced the solemn practice of handing over the creed to the elect, it is also anomalous for catechumens who have not been "given" the text of the creed to be present when the community proclaims it. It is therefore clear that the catechumens should be dismissed before the profession of faith and the eucharistic prayer. There still are a variety of practices, however, concerning the suitable point at which catechumens leave the assembly.

In the RCIA there are several references to an appropriate order for dismissing the catechumens (for example, #68, 117, 156, 170 in the U.S. edition), with some room for adaptations. After giving texts for intercessions for the catechumens and for their dismissal, the basic rubric (#68, from the rite of acceptance) reads:

> When the eucharist is to follow, intercessory prayer is resumed [after the catechumens leave] with the usual general intercessions for the needs of the church and the whole world; then, if required, the profession of faith is said. But for pastoral reasons these general intercessions and the profession of faith may be omitted. The liturgy of the eucharist then begins as usual with the preparation of gifts.

Thus the complete order is that after the homily (1) the assembly prays for the catechumens; (2) the catechumens are dismissed; (3) the assembly engages in the priestly prayer of interceding for the needs of the world; (4) the profession of faith is proclaimed and (5) the eucharist is celebrated.

This order is not really a modern invention. It is basically the same pattern that has been used for centuries in Byzantine churches. In the complete form of the Byzantine liturgy, there is an "insistent litany" after the homily, and then the litany for the catechumens and their dismissal. Only after the dismissal of the catechumens are the two "litanies of the faithful" sung. And in the Byzantine liturgy, the Nicene Creed is sung later, after the gifts have been brought to the altar and immediately before the eucharistic prayer.

One might question the appropriateness of duplicating litanies, given that the reforms of Vatican II tried to eliminate unnecessary duplications. Perhaps by focusing on what may appear unrelated—a rubric in the Easter Vigil—some insight can be gained into the values of the complete order.

At the Easter Vigil, the last rubric at the end of the liturgy of baptism is worded in an interesting way: "After the people have been sprinkled, the priest returns to the chair. The profession of faith is omitted, and the priest directs the general intercessions, in which the newly baptized take part for the first time."

This rubric points to an ancient principle that is sometimes overlooked: Participating in intercessory prayer is a priestly action performed by the baptized; those who are not baptized, and thus are not part of the priestly people that constitutes Christ's body, cannot participate in that prayer. The alternative title for the "general intercessions" is the "prayer of the faithful," with "faithful" indicating the assembly of the baptized. Only after their initiation should candidates be present for and fully participate in the intercessory prayer of the assembled church.

A full ritual dismissal would come between two forms of prayer—one by the assembly for the catechumens before their dismissal and one by the assembly for the needs of the world after the catechumens leave. The first set of intercessions is primarily for the catechumens (or, later, the elect), and that litany concludes with a prayer for those preparing for initiation and a general or individual imposition of hands by the presiding priest. On those occasions when the standard set of intercessions is omitted, it is permitted to include general petitions for the church and the world within the intercessions for the catechumens. But those additional intercessions should not change the focus of that litany, which remains a prayer for the catechumens or the elect.

It is important to maintain the distinction. To blend two different litanies into one in this case can denigrate the significance of the standard "general intercessions." Christians need to realize that it is a sacred moment when we participate in prayer for our world, in imitation of our Master. It is our birthright given to us by rebirth in baptism. When separate intercessions, in which only the baptized participate, are regularly omitted from the Sunday liturgy, the significance of the first participation by the newly initiated at the Easter Vigil amounts to nothing. Instead, this first participation in intercessory prayer should be seen as another step in the initiation ritual—washed and anointed, before sharing in the sacred meal, the neophytes join the community as Christians and exercise their Christian duty in praying for the needs of the world, and then in bringing the bread and wine to the altar for the eucharist. The importance and significance of participating in such a prayer is, unfortunately, often overlooked—but it should never be trivialized.

Thus I recommend that two litanies always be used—a shorter one specifically for the catechumens, after which they are dismissed, followed by the standard general intercessions, the priestly prayer of the baptized assembly.

Liturgy of the Eucharist

Should the money that is collected in the assembly at Mass be presented with the bread and wine, or should it be collected while the bread and wine are presented and then quietly taken out for safe keeping?

In describing the presentation of the gifts and the altar, the 2000 *General Instruction of the Roman Missal* (#73) explicitly makes mention of "money or other gifts . . . brought in by the faithful or collected" at the Mass. It states that they are brought forward along with the bread and wine for the eucharist and are received by the priest and deacon. A few paragraphs later, the GIRM states that "the faithful's participation" in the preparations of the gifts is "expressed by their presenting both the bread and wine . . . and other gifts to meet the needs of the church and of the poor" (#140).

Thus the guidelines for the typical format of a Sunday Mass given by GIRM assume that the money collected will be brought up with the bread and wine in one procession and presented to the priest who accepts them, preparing and then placing the bread and the wine on the altar. The only caveat given by GIRM is that money or other gifts for the poor should not be placed on the altar but put in some other suitable place (2000 GIRM, 73 and 140).

Parishes who follow the prescriptions of GIRM usually arrange the preparation of the gifts in this way: After the general intercessions, all sit (including the presiding priest) as the song at the presentation begins. Then the ushers take up the collection and the servers prepare the altar by placing upon it the sacramentary, corporal, purificator and chalice. Usually after a verse or two of the song, the collection is finished and the procession takes place with the bread, wine and money. The bread and wine are taken to the altar and placed there (with the accompanying prayers being said *inaudibly*), while the money is taken and placed in a safe location away from the altar — near the credence table or even in a secure location in the sacristy.

The current directions in the GIRM regarding the collection are an attempt to integrate this activity into the entire eucharistic action. The collection should not be seen as an interruption in the flow of the liturgy or a necessary evil that is going on simultaneously while the priest continues with the Mass. It is a way for all in the assembly to contribute to the community, as the assembly historically did through bringing bread, water and wine.

Extraneous concerns seem to convince parish staff sometimes to imitate the practice common prior to Vatican II — that the collection takes place *while* the priest prepares the gifts at the altar, after the procession with the bread and wine. Sometimes the argument is given that it is foolhardy to leave a large amount of money in the open in the sanctuary or that postponing the procession with the gifts until after the collection would unduly prolong the liturgy. I think both of these valid concerns can be dealt with in other ways. For example, it is possible for an usher to bring up the collection in the procession with the gifts, present it to the presider and then be entrusted with it to be taken to a safe place. If time is really a major concern, perhaps more ushers should be used to take up the collection, or the scheduling of Masses should be examined by the parish staff so that liturgical principles are not compromised too readily, or perhaps other secondary practices that lengthen the liturgy needlessly need to be looked at.

As with other elements of our eucharistic liturgy, there is a constant challenge that each element be integrated into a well-ordered whole and not seem to be extraneous to the action taking place. In some situations, it might be necessary to adapt an ideal described in the GIRM, but those ideals, based on solid liturgical principles, should never be merely ignored.

I've noticed that in church-goods catalogs extra large hosts, perhaps six inches in diameter, are available. Are these just another liturgical fad, like intinction cups, or is there something that I'm overlooking that suggests their use? Could you offer some guidance?

Old habits are hard to break. The present *Order of Mass* and *the General Instruction of the Roman Missal* were published in 1969, and only recently have people taken notice of some of their implications. Paragraph 321 of the 2000 GIRM states the following: "The nature of the sign demands that the material for the eucharistic celebration truly have the appearance of food." Ideally, churches of the Roman Rite should use home-baked bread, as Catholics of Byzantine churches do. Dennis Krouse's recipe of wheat, flour and water (see Gabe Huck's *The Communion Rite at Sunday Mass,* p. 78; *Liturgy 80,* October 1986, p. 12) is particularly easy to use and produces a bread that smells, tastes and looks like real food. The same reasons that urge communion under both kinds also urge the use of home-baked eucharistic bread. Those who suggest otherwise are unconsciously down-playing sacramental authenticity at the expense of efficiency or an outdated piety.

It may take time for some to move from wafer bread (that is, hosts) toward more substantial forms of bread. Meanwhile, eucharistic practice must still be guided by the GIRM: "It is desirable that the eucharistic bread be made in such a way that . . . the priest is able actually to break the host into parts and distribute them to at least some of the faithful" (#321). This stresses the importance of the union of those present through their sharing in the one bread.

Unfortunately, it is a common practice at Mass (based on the rubrics of the Tridentine Missal) for the priest to use, break and entirely consume a larger host (about two inches in diameter), while the people receive smaller hosts (about one inch in diameter). Even at concelebrations, the bread is sometimes prepared so that each concelebrating priest is allotted a separate larger host and consumes both halves at communion as if he were saying Mass by himself. The GIRM, however, provides no basis for continuing these older practices of having separate different sized hosts for priests alone. In fact, the 2000 GIRM suggests a contrary practice as the norm; it refers to "bread for the communion of the priest," but it also says "the ministers, and the people" suggesting one loaf for many people (2000 GIRM, 118c). In the *Order of Mass,* the rubrics mention only "bread" without referring to size or distinguishing between priest and people.

Given the renewed importance of the "breaking of the bread" (see Acts 2:42), the importance of the unity of the assembly through sharing the one bread (see 1 Corinthians 10:17) and the importance of always consecrating enough bread at Mass for the communicants present (2000 GIRM, 85), it is most desirable to make use of home-baked bread or, as a second choice, of hosts much larger than the two-inch size widely used. Thus, if home-baked bread is unavailable, hosts at least the size of the six-inch host ("paten size" or "concelebration size") should be the bread normally used at Mass. One version of these extra-large hosts is scored to break easily into twenty-four particles. These extra-large hosts, though still not ideal, are more in keeping with both the spirit and the letter of the revised Missal. For typical weekday Masses, there should be no need for using one-inch hosts. At larger gatherings, such as on Sundays, the use of small hosts is permitted, but these should not be used in lieu of "paten size" hosts, but only to supplement them (2000 GIRM, 321). The use of several "paten size" hosts at both Sunday and weekday Masses would also enhance the rite of the breaking of the bread rather than retaining a minimal, perfunctory action of breaking one two-inch host into two pieces.

The significance of the broken bread also suggests that when the assembly is invited to communion ("This is the Lamb of

God . . ."), a single broken piece of bread should be raised over the chalice (2000 GIRM, 157). The presiding priest should not try to piece a host together, pretending as if it were not broken. It is the broken bread that the people are invited to share, and this is what they should be shown.

I would envision only two occasions for which the "traditional" two-inch size "large" host would be used: (1) when a host is needed for exposition in a monstrance, and (2) when a very small congregation is present (for example, two or three people other than the priest). In all other cases, home-baked bread or, if necessary, one or more "paten size" hosts should be the norm.

What is the role of music in the preparation of the gifts at Sunday Mass? Should the assembly sing? Should the choir? Should there be instrumental music or no music at all?

The preparation of the gifts is a simple action that is both secondary and preliminary to the eucharistic prayer. The complete rite of preparing the altar and the gifts consists of (1) preparing the altar, (2) bringing the gifts in procession to the altar, (3) placing the gifts on the altar (after saying the "Blessed are you" prayers), (4) incensing both the gifts and the people and washing the presider's hands and (5) saying the prayer over the gifts. If music or song is used during this part of the liturgy, it should begin while the altar is being prepared (2000 GIRM, 139), and it should continue until after the gifts are placed on the altar, that is, until the prayer over the gifts (2000 GIRM, 74).

The basic principle that should determine whether to employ music and what type of music to use is a consideration of the relative importance of the preparation of the gifts to other parts of the liturgy. Preparing the gifts is preliminary to their sanctification in the eucharistic prayer and this secondary nature should be reflected in any choices made about music. It is misdirected, for example, to prepare the choir to sing a complicated motet yet not give proper attention to singing the responsorial psalm, the gospel acclamation, the eucharistic prayer or at least its acclamations. One should never emphasize the secondary while neglecting the primary.

Music in Catholic Worship (issued by the U.S. Bishops' Committee on the Liturgy in 1972) offers other points for consideration. It notes that a song during the preparation of the gifts "is not always necessary or desirable," and when used, "it need not speak of bread and wine or of offering" (#71). It also notes that if a song is sung, the "proper function of this song is to accompany and celebrate the communal aspects of the procession" with the gifts, but that "organ or instrumental music is also fitting." Elsewhere it states that for this or similar optional songs (such as the hymn after communion or the recessional), "there is no question of usurping the people's parts" so that "the choir may play a further role" (#70).

Mass tends to be a very wordy affair. The preparation of the gifts comes after three biblical readings (and the psalm), the homily, the creed and the intercessions. Emotionally, this part of the liturgy might be an appropriate moment to have silence (perhaps even having the presiding priest recite all his preparation prayers inaudibly) so that the assembly can reflect on the word and prepare for the actions of the eucharistic prayer and the communion rite.

An alternative is instrumental music, or a subdued hymn sung by the cantor or the choir, that aids reflection rather than drawing attention to itself. The members of the assembly may need to have free hands to prepare their money offerings or other gifts for the poor, especially in those parishes where baskets are passed hand to hand. If the assembly sings at the preparation, some of the quieter Taize canons might be appropriate. The choir can play a leading role (but not an exclusive or overpowering one) by singing in parts.

There are many options for music during this point of the Mass. Mindful of the secondary nature of the preparation of the gifts, the appropriate choice should be made in context of what else is sung during the liturgy, the ability of the assembly, the quality and skill of the music ministry and even the season of the year or the nature of the particular feast.

Where should the presiding priest receive the gifts brought up in the procession at the presentation of the gifts?

The 2000 *General Instruction of the Roman Missal,* when describing this moment of the Mass, merely states that the gifts are "accepted at an appropriate place by the priest or deacon" (#73). Other paragraphs of the GIRM (for example, #140 and 178) do not offer any further guidance, and paragraph 145 of the *Ceremonial of Bishops* merely reiterates the "appropriate place" of the GIRM.

It is customary in many places, after the general intercessions and the collection, for the priest (accompanied by the deacon and one or more servers) to leave the chair and go to the edge of the sanctuary to a location close to where he stands to distribute communion. There he receives the gifts of bread and wine along with the collection and other offerings for the poor. In older churches, this often is the place where the "gate" of the sanctuary rail used to (or might still) be.

Some, however, have questioned the "appropriateness" of this location. Even though it might be convenient for those bringing up the gifts (allowing them to avoid ascending several steps into the central sanctuary area), one can argue that receiving the gifts here suggests that those who bring up the gifts of bread and wine should not get too close to the altar. Receiving the gifts where the "sanctuary gate" might have been (or might still be) subtly reinforces the notion that the laity should not enter the "sanctuary." Even though the physical sanctuary rail may no longer exist in many churches, a psychological barrier may still be in place.

If one reflects on televised papal Masses when the pope travels around the world, it is not unusual to see the Holy Father remaining seated at his chair during this part of the liturgy. One will usually see those participating in the procession with the gifts walking up the stairs of the platform on which the altar is located, then past the altar to the presidential chair and handing the gifts from the people of God to the pope at the chair. The pope then hands the various gifts to assisting deacons or servers, who either hold them at the altar until needed or place them in the appropriate locations. Thus there is papal precedent for receiving gifts at a place other than the sanctuary's edge.

One can view the procession with the gifts as the first "movement" of a multipartite action that climaxes with the physical placement of the bread and wine on the altar and concludes with the prayer over the gifts. Thus the location at which the presiding priest accepts the gifts can help (or hinder) the assembly's understanding of what this part of the Mass is ultimately all about, and it can help (or hinder) the assembly to see its intrinsic unity.

The liturgy of the eucharist is structured to follow the actions and words of Christ at the Last Supper (2000 GIRM, 72), often summarized with the four verbs of take, bless, break and share. And the first action mentioned in the various scriptural accounts is that Christ took bread and wine. Thus, the presentation of the gifts corresponds to this action of Jesus. The ritual activity reaches its high point when the priest receives the bread and wine into his hands and then reverently places them on the corporal, where they come into physical contact with the altar, the architectural symbol of Christ in each church (2000 GIRM, 298). The "Blessed are you . . ." prayers imitate Jewish tradition in that usually no special food is taken without God being praised. But ultimately these prayers are secondary to the action of reverently placing the bread and wine on the altar. In fact, some have suggested that the priest should be permitted to omit these prayers entirely (and not merely recite them inaudibly) so that he can join the assembly in song.

A careful reading of the rubrics of the sacramentary and of the text of the GIRM indicates that there is no justification for the all-too-common practice of a priest receiving the bread and wine, placing them on the altar, lifting each high in the air while saying the prayer and then placing them on the altar a second time. Placing the eucharistic elements on the altar is an action that should be done once and only once!

We should also note that the GIRM gives no support to the pre-Vatican II understanding of this section of the liturgy as being an "offertory." The only "offering" takes place after the institution narrative (what we used to call "the consecration") during the eucharistic prayer (see 2000 GIRM, 79f).

A typical ritual pattern found in the Roman liturgical tradition is that processions are formally concluded with a solemn prayer. Hence, the entrance procession (and the opening rite of the Mass) is concluded by an opening prayer, and the communion procession (and meditation after communion) is concluded by the prayer after communion. Thus one can construe the prayer over the gifts as the formal conclusion to the procession with the gifts and the preparation and placement of the bread and wine on the altar.

Given this background and this understanding of the preparation of the gifts, what would be an alternative "appropriate place," that is also liturgically significant, for the priest to receive the gifts of bread and wine?

Some churches have found the following choreography appropriate, and I offer it for reflection and possible adoption or adaptation.

When the procession with the gifts begins, the priest and deacon immediately approach the altar, standing where they normally stand during the eucharistic prayer, perhaps a few feet further back. Those carrying the bread and wine ascend the steps of the "sanctuary" and approach the priest and deacon where they stand. The bearers of the bread and wine can approach together from the same side or can separate and approach from opposite sides of the altar.

The deacon receives the container of wine and immediately goes to the credence table to add water to the container and pour some wine into a chalice (2000 GIRM, 178). Meanwhile, the priest receives the container of bread, immediately says the "Blessed are you . . ." prayer inaudibly while holding the vessel only "slightly" above the altar, and then reverently places the vessel with bread on the altar (2000 GIRM, 141). Those presenting the gifts may stand behind the priest for the moment. The deacon brings the chalice and the flagon or carafe back to the priest and hands them to him (but does not place them on the altar himself). The priest receives the wine, says the prayer and reverently places the wine on the altar. (Note that the bread and wine do not make physical contact with the altar until the priest has finished each prescribed prayer.)

After the other prayers, the incensation and the washing of hands, the priest brings this portion of the liturgy of the eucharist to a conclusion with the prayer over the gifts. Those who presented the gifts then return to their places.

Ultimately, the preparation of the gifts, as well as the breaking of the bread, even though they are significant points of the liturgy of the eucharist, are really preparatory and secondary to the eucharistic prayer and the reception of communion. But being a secondary activity does not mean that the action is insignificant or that the action can be executed perfunctorily. How the bread and wine are handled, where they are received and how they are placed on the altar all reflect how the assembly and its presider understand what is happening at this point in the liturgy. Each can contribute to or detract from the entire action of giving thanks and praise to God.

What prefaces can be used with the eucharistic prayers for Masses of reconciliation and Masses with children? Why do some prayers have fixed prefaces and some have variable ones?

The simple answer to the first question is that all those eucharistic prayers mentioned have their own prefaces and those prefaces are the only ones meant to be used with those prayers. But why?

There are two major traditions regarding eucharistic prayers. One employs multiple eucharistic prayers, each composed as a single literary unit. The other uses a single eucharistic prayer with certain sections fixed and other sections variable.

The present sacramentary includes eucharistic prayers based on both traditions. The tradition of multiple prayers with unchangeable parts has given rise to Eucharistic Prayer IV, the two Eucharistic Prayers for Reconciliation and Eucharistic Prayers I and II for Masses with Children. The tradition of combining a fixed text with certain variable sections is the norm for Eucharistic Prayers I and III and Eucharistic Prayer III for Children, as well as the Eucharistic Prayer for Various Needs and Occasions. Eucharistic Prayer II has its own preface, but other prefaces also can be used, thereby bridging both traditions (2000 GIRM, 365b).

The tradition of multiple prayers with unchangeable parts is related to the literary integrity of the prayer. Such prayers were composed under the assumption that they would always be prayed in their entirety—without any textual substitutions for major sections. For example, in Eucharistic Prayer IV, the preface praises God for all creation. The first mention of Jesus does not occur until several sentences after the Sanctus during the proclamation of salvation history. It would do damage to the literary integrity and internal coherence of the text to substitute another preface in the sacramentary for the preface that is integral to that prayer. One doesn't mix and match sections of Shakesperean sonnets simply for variety, because that would violate the integrity and coherence of those poems as they were conceived by the author. Similarly, eucharistic prayers intended as self-contained literary works should only be used in their entirety.

Since the eucharistic prayers for reconciliation and those for children are recent additions to the sacramentary, precise rules regarding their use are not found in the GIRM. However, the 1974 decrees accompanying their publication imply that they are similar to Eucharistic Prayer IV, that is, they were written as self-contained prayers. For this reason, that integrity should be respected and no other preface in the sacramentary should be substituted (2000 GIRM, 365d). Eucharistic Prayer for Masses with Children III has a special preface, a post-Sanctus section and intercessions for the Easter Season. One should respect the literary integrity of this prayer as well and use it only with the texts specially prepared for the prayer.

Thus, at present, the corpus of over eighty prefaces in the sacramentary may only be used with Eucharistic Prayers I, II and III. Proper prefaces should be used (in conjunction with these three prayers) whenever there is a special mention of the celebration, for example, at ritual masses (such as weddings), on major feasts (such as December 8, November 1, June 29) or on special liturgical days (such as octaves of Christmas and Easter, Sundays of Lent in Year A). Aside from those occasions and especially during Ordinary Time and on all weekdays of any liturgical season, the other eucharistic prayers (with their own fixed prefaces) may be used whenever appropriate, such as reconciliation prayers during Lent or Eucharistic Prayer IV during Easter.

What's the best way to decide which eucharistic prayer to use on a given Sunday?

The eucharistic prayer is the most important of all the presidential prayers of the Mass (2000 GIRM, 30 and 78), yet often people overlook it when preparing liturgies. In the United States, there are ten options in the English-language sacramentary to choose from: Eucharistic Prayers I, II, III and IV; two eucharistic prayers for reconciliation; three eucharistic prayers for Masses with children; and then the eucharistic prayer for various needs and occasions, with four particular prefaces and intercessory sections.

In one sense, because the basic content of the eucharistic prayer remains constant—praise and thanks to God for salvation through the death and resurrection of Jesus—there is no need to change the text at every Mass. Yet repetition of a single text can be deadening. Thus it is good to use all legitimate options, making choices based on a set of criteria rather than on a mental flip of a coin after the prayer over the gifts.

Some possible criteria are based on the internal nature and content of the various prayers. For example, because of its length and peculiar literary structure, Eucharistic Prayer I (the Roman Canon) is not a good candidate for typical Sunday celebrations. It includes lengthy intercessions and almost no element of praise or thanksgiving. On the other hand, it does include special insertions for major feasts—so this prayer might be appropriate on such feasts or on the feast of some saint named in its intercessions.

Eucharistic Prayer II, based on a third-century prayer by Saint Hippolytus of Rome, is generally too short for Sundays, but might be appropriate if sung. Eucharistic Prayer III is of an appropriate length and content, but repeated use can harm its overall effectiveness. Eucharistic Prayer IV must be used with its own preface, but it includes a very good proclamation of salvation history, which provides an excellent context for praise and thanksgiving. It also includes phrases from the gospel of John and might well be used to echo some aspect of the day's gospel. The two prayers for reconciliation contain sentiments that make them appropriate for the season of Lent, but they can also be used profitably whenever the scriptures speak about forgiveness and reconciliation. The second prayer is a good choice for times of civil unrest, so we can pray that "in the midst of conflict and division . . . you turn our minds to thoughts of peace."

Other criteria for choosing an appropriate eucharistic prayer are based on external considerations. For example, if a proper preface is assigned to a specific Sunday (certain Sundays of Lent), the choice is limited to Eucharistic Prayers I, II and III, because the other seven prayers must be used with their own prefaces. If children constitute a significant portion of the assembly, one of the three prayers for Masses with children could be used.

Choosing the prayer text is only one element in making this section of the liturgy come alive. One should also consider singing and posture. The norm is that the Sanctus, the Memorial Acclamation and the Amen are always sung, and in many parishes this does happen. Many parts of the priest's text, however, could also be sung. Indeed, the whole prayer could be sung. There are simple chants in the sacramentary, and contemporary settings of the entire eucharistic prayer have been published. Regarding posture, some communities have experimented with standing for the entire prayer, because changing posture after the Sanctus suggests that the eucharistic prayer is not really a unity.

Because this prayer is the center of the Sunday assembly, every effort should be made to enhance its celebration. Something is off balance when people experience the Lord's Prayer or the sign of peace as more important than the eucharistic prayer. Choosing an appropriate text from among the legitimate options in the sacramentary should be part of the overall planning, but it is only one aspect of celebrating the liturgy well.

How should the bread and cup be held during the doxology at the end of the eucharistic prayer?

The gestures of the priest with the bread and cup during the doxology of the eucharistic prayer have been modified several times over the last few decades. In the 1570 Roman Missal (used until the interim revisions of the 1960s), the priest, while inaudibly reciting the majority of the doxology, made three signs of the cross with the host over the chalice, then two more with the host between the chalice and himself and then finally slightly elevated the chalice with the host over it before concluding the doxology audibly and beginning the introduction to the Lord's Prayer.

The interim simplification of the rubrics in the mid-1960s, immediately after the Second Vatican Council, omitted all the signs of the cross and prescribed that the priest should hold the host (in his right hand) over the chalice (in his left hand) and elevate both slightly while saying all of the doxology aloud.

The 1969 *Order of Mass* significantly changed the rubrics for the doxology. Dropped is any mention of lifting the bread and cup only "slightly," and the verb used, *elevans,* is the one used in the former missal to describe the "elevation" after the words of consecration. In other words, this "elevation" has regained its original stature as the great elevation followed by the great Amen. Also significant is the fact that the bread is now to remain on the paten (horizontally) during the doxology and is not to be held over the cup (vertically).

Unfortunately, the rubric, as printed before the doxology in the *Order of Mass* in the sacramentary, is one of a few "incompletely" revised rubrics in the current liturgical books and may lead to some confusion. Almost every other rubric currently in the Order of Mass takes into account the role of the deacon according to the provisions of the *General Instruction of the Roman Missal* (#171–186). But the rubric printed at the words of the doxology omits the role of the deacon as described in GIRM (#180).

According to the 2000 GIRM, the normative gestures at the doxology involve two people (priest and deacon) holding up the two eucharistic species, each in its own vessel—the bread on the plate, the wine in the cup (#180). When a deacon is present—the traditional minister of the cup—he stands next to the priest and lifts up the cup during the doxology. The priest takes the plate with the consecrated bread and lifts it up while singing or saying the doxology. After the people have finished the Amen, the plate and cup are placed again on the altar. If there is no deacon, a concelebrating priest may lift up the cup, but only one plate and one cup should be lifted during the doxology. Additional vessels should remain on the altar even if several deacons or concelebrants are present. If there is no deacon (or concelebrant), the priest adapts the normative gesture by holding both vessels.

Elevating the consecrated elements during the doxology is one of the oldest gestures during the eucharistic prayer in the Roman tradition. (The "elevations" after the consecration are much more recent.) The current practice is modeled after the seventh-century practice of Rome, in which a deacon (at papal Masses) would hold up the cup and the pope would lift two loaves of bread. The twentieth-century liturgist Joseph Jungmann, SJ, saw this gesture as an offering of the elements to God rather than as a showing of the elements to the people. As the eucharistic prayer is brought to a conclusion, the presiding priest proclaims that "all glory and honor" is given "through . . . with . . . and in" Christ to our Almighty Father, and that this lifting up of "all glory and honor" through Christ to God is indicated in gesture by the lifting up of the consecrated elements.

It is not uncommon, however, to find the former practice (holding the host vertically over the chalice) still depicted in art or even practiced by some priests. This is unfortunate for two reasons.

First, continuing the former gesture reinforces a bygone piety and suggests that the revised gesture in the current *Order of Mass* is not as good as the one it replaced. There may be deficiencies in the current *Order of Mass* and room for further development, but I am unwilling to suggest that "improvement" is achieved by reintroducing old rubrics that were deliberately changed!

Second, the former gesture is basically an unnatural one. In our society, we do not hold solid food over liquids. It is not unnatural for people to hold a cup or glass in one hand and a plate in the other, and it is also not unnatural for people to raise up a glass (in a toast). But on reflection, the gesture of holding a piece of bread over a cup of wine has no relationship to anything normally done with food and drink in our society.

The only time I could envision modifying the rubric in the *Order of Mass* is when there is no deacon (or concelebrant) and there is only a very large single vessel holding all the bread for the eucharist (a practice that has much to recommend itself in terms of the sign value of the sacrament of unity). It might be awkward or very difficult for the priest to lift up this vessel in one hand and hold the cup in the other. In this case only, the priest might lift a large consecrated bread out of the vessel, keeping it flat on the palm of one hand while holding the cup in his other hand. Yet even in this case, the gesture should model the normative gesture as much as possible and avoid any imitation of the gesture of the 1570 missal.

What are the pros and cons of joining hands during the Our Father?

The question of whether it is good for all present at Mass to hold hands during the Our Father has been discussed for quite a while. In the early 1970s, the Roman Congregation for Divine Worship was asked whether joining hands during the Lord's Prayer could take the place of the formal exchange of peace. In 1975 a response suggested that the "prolonged holding of hands" is a "sign of communion rather than of peace" and that it should not substitute for the official "sign of peace [which] is filled with meaning, graciousness and Christian inspiration." The response said that, in general, it did not seem right to substitute for the sign of peace "a different gesture with less meaning into another part of the Mass" (*Notitiae* 11 (1975), p. 226 [DOL, 1502 footnote R29]).

This answer suggests that the prolonged holding of hands during the Our Father is a different action than the brief gesture of greeting and touch that normally constitutes the sign of peace. The response also suggests that it is wrong to substitute the new prolonged gesture for the official brief gesture. The answer, however, did not forbid the practice in itself if it were performed in addition to the normal exchange of the sign of peace.

In his wonderful little book, *Preparing for Liturgy,* Austin Fleming suggests that this gesture (and other similar "new traditions") bears some reflection and raises some questions. One question asks, "Have we considered the fact that one must drop the hands of one sign of unity in order the shake the hand just dropped in another sign of unity?"

Other points about this practice should be considered. This gesture is without precedent in the history of the Roman rite and is not envisioned by the rubrics. Yet when it is used, it is demanded of everyone present at Mass. Many people may feel awkward or angry about being forced to participate in such a gesture. How does one graciously say, "No, thank you," when someone grabs your hand and intends to hold on for the duration of the prayer? No other similar gesture is demanded of everyone. No one is forced to make the sign of the cross at the beginning or the end of the Mass. Not everyone present need receive communion. Some may be seated during the silence after communion while others stand or kneel. Yet holding hands at the Our Father admits of few exceptions.

This gesture can be criticized also on the grounds that it is inappropriate for prayer. An ancient posture of prayer is the *orans* position, in which one stands with arms outstretched and raised, palms opened upward. In former times, entire assemblies prayed in this fashion. This is the gesture now used by the presider during the presidential prayers. The revised Italian sacramentary permits all in the assembly to extend their hands during the Lord's Prayer in this ancient gesture. Perhaps this alternative gesture should be given more of a chance in other parts of the world as well. Holding hands is not a traditional gesture of prayer. In contrast, it is associated with love and solidarity, with a young couple on a date, with a group of people trying to establish unity and singing a song of unity.

I recognize that holding hands for the Lord's Prayer has helped create a communal experience at liturgy in some parishes in a way that little else has managed to do. Yet I also think it is an inappropriate response to the situation where people "don't feel like a community." Community and solidarity are to be our stance throughout the entire liturgy and are expressed most fully in our walking together to the table, in our singing of the communion song and in our sharing of the bread and the cup. More catechesis on these parts of the liturgy is needed. In other words, what people are looking for is already in the liturgy, just waiting to be experienced and "opened up." Of course, these parts of the ritual require thoughtful preparation and well-trained ministers and musicians for people to be able to experience the full meaning of the communion rite.

I would not suggest that holding hands at the Our Father should be dropped immediately in those places where it has become well established. Stopping the practice could be detrimental to those to whom it has become meaningful. It will be difficult to explain eliminating a gesture that was introduced as a sign of unity. Yet I think that no one should be compelled to participate in this gesture. How one communicates this option is a mystery to me, however, because for holding hands to be a sign of unity, all must participate. That is another reason why I question its appropriateness. I would not advocate that holding hands be introduced in places where it is unknown. If a gesture is felt to be needed, perhaps the *orans* posture should be tried, a gesture with a two thousand-year tradition of use within Christian prayer.

Attempts to help assemblies experience that all present are brothers and sisters in Christ should be encouraged. Yet we must seriously reflect on innovations in our liturgy. One of the goals of the post-Vatican II liturgical revisions was to remove elements that were ill-suited to the role they were actually playing in the rite. It would be too bad if new gestures (that may not all be well thought out) were introduced into the liturgy when we have not really made use of, savored and seen the great potential of the existing words and gestures.

Is it permissible to skip the sign of peace at Mass? If so, is it advisable? Some people think it's a break in the ritual to say, "How do you do?" while others think it's a disrespectful commotion before communion. Most simply don't understand it. How do I address these attitudes?

Among the Eastern and Western Catholic churches, the sign of peace appears in various places during the Mass. For example, in the Ambrosian liturgy of Milan, the exchange of peace usually occurs before the gifts are brought to the altar and thus before the taking/blessing/breaking/sharing of the gifts—the fourfold shape of the classic celebration. In the Byzantine liturgy, the exchange of peace occurs after the gifts have been placed on the altar but before the Nicene Creed and the eucharistic prayer. In such a location, it follows the "taking" of the eucharistic elements but does not interrupt the dynamics of the liturgical action by occurring anywhere between "blessing" the holy bread and wine, and "breaking" the bread and "sharing" the elements in communion.

For many people, the exchange of peace as it occurs in the Roman Mass—between the eucharistic prayer and the breaking of the bread—does seem to interrupt the flow of this section of the liturgy. Yet it might not really be as much of an interruption as it first might seem.

The location of the sign of peace in the Roman tradition is usually explained by its relationship to what precedes it (the Lord's Prayer) as well as to what follows it (the breaking of the bread and the sharing of communion). In the Lord's prayer, we ask the Father to forgive us "as we forgive those who trespass against us." And in the embolism, the presider prays to God: "Grant us peace in our day." It can be considered quite appropriate to turn these prayer-sentiments into a concrete liturgical action. By greeting others with

Christ's peace, all in the assembly can show that they are attempting reconciliation with others and that they are willing to extend the peace that they beg God to grant our world.

The 2000 *General Instruction of the Roman Missal* also links the exchange of peace to the liturgical actions that follow it (#82). The next paragraph refers to the words of Saint Paul in reminding us of a symbolic aspect of the breaking of the bread: that those who partake of the one loaf are made one in the Christ (following 1 Corinthians 10:17). In preparation for being united through sharing the body and blood of Christ in communion, the sign of peace is seen as a sign of love and unity, and thus as a way to remind those assembled that the eucharist is also a sacrament of unity.

Years ago, I heard a bishop comment on the sign of peace in yet another way. Sharing the sign of peace with others and receiving it as well was, for him, an acknowledgment of Christ's presence in them. After all, Saint Paul reminds us that we are the body of Christ (1 Corinthians 12:27). The bishop saw the sign of peace as a very appropriate means through which we publicly reverence Christ's presence in our neighbor before approaching the eucharistic table, where we acknowledge Christ's presence in the eucharistic bread and wine. Both dimensions are necessary for a well-balanced spirituality. Given these various interpretations of the meaning of the sign of peace, it seems right to share it at every Mass. Yet this is not universally done.

Part of the problem may be a misunderstanding of the nature of this ritual action and a distaste for the way it is practiced in the local community. The sign of peace is definitely not a time for "Hello, how are you?" greetings but is rather a time of prayerful sharing of Christ's peace, love and unity. Everyone in the assembly should briefly greet those nearest them immediately after the presiding priest has greeted the assembly.

For the priest to wander down the aisle is to suggest a clerical interpretation of the rite, as if one could not find Christ in one's neighbor unless one received Christ's peace from the presider first. Moreover, the 2000 GIRM specifies that the priest should remain in the sanctuary "so as not to disturb the celebration" (2000 GIRM,

154). In addition, for members of the assembly to feel compelled to greet many people (or everyone else present in small groups) is also to misinterpret the nature of this ritual action and to prolong it so that it overwhelms more important parts of the liturgy. Both these variations on the rite distort the stark simplicity of this gesture and the nature of this liturgical action, and so are best avoided.

The exchange of peace is the only ritual moment in the Roman Mass in which members of the assembly explicitly acknowledge other members of the assembly rather than respond to the presiding priest or to other ministers. If it is understood as flowing from the words of the Lord's prayer and anticipating the unity that we try to achieve through communion, it would seem that people would be eager to share Christ's peace ritually.

Omitting the sign of peace comes from a misreading of the text of the sacramentary. The rubric before the exchange of peace states that the deacon may *(pro opportunitate)* say: "Let us offer each other a sign of peace." But the following rubric, "All offer one another a sign that expresses peace, communion and charity" (2000 GIRM, 154), does not include any of the typical words that usually occur if something is left to the discretion of the presiding priest (see 2000 GIRM, 164). In the directions for concelebrated Masses, the 2000 GIRM plainly (without any hint of there being an option) states that "all exchange the sign of peace" (#239). In other words, the rubrics state that the invitation to the exchange of peace, "Let us offer . . . ," is optional; but literally, the rubrics make no mention of any option being associated with the actual rite itself.

Some priests have interpreted the "may" of the invitation also to apply to the actual exchange of peace. Thus they omit it, occasionally or even regularly. Yet more recent liturgical books, such as the *Ceremonial of Bishops,* word the rubrics to indicate that it is only the invitation to the exchange of peace that is optional (CB, 161; see also #99–103).

The optional nature of the diaconal invitation is also found in other places in the sacramentary, for example, for the solemn blessing. In the general description of the parts of the Mass found in the GIRM (#46–90), the text speaks of the homily as being "recommended" on weekdays (#66) and that it is "desirable" that the general intercessions be included at all Masses with a congregation (#69). But there is no such tentativeness regarding the sign of peace (#82). It is true that the rubrics say that the priest "may" exchange a sign of peace with the ministers (2000 GIRM, 154), but this exchange by the presider is optional since it, in effect, duplicates the first greeting of peace that the priest has just extended to everyone in the assembly, including the ministers near the altar. (When the bishop celebrates, the rubrics require that he exchange a sign of peace with at least the two nearest concelebrants and one of the deacons.)

The gospel of John records that the night before Christ died, he prayed for unity (John 17) and gave his gift of peace to his disciples (John 14:27). Most postresurrection apparitions of Christ record that the Lord greeted his disciples with the words "Peace be with you" (John 20:19). As we approach the eucharistic banquet that the risen Lord has prepared for us, it is most appropriate that we share his peace with those nearest us in the assembly. This is not something that should be seen as either an option or an interruption. Rather, it is something at the core of Christ's message for his followers.

When should the communion song begin? When should eucharistic ministers and other ministers receive communion?

Paragraph 86 of the 2000 *General Instruction of the Roman Missal* states that singing at communion begins during the priest's reception of the sacrament. (See also 2000 GIRM, 159.) It also states that the "singing continues while the faithful receive the sacrament." Thus the communion song should begin immediately after the response of the assembly, "Lord, I am not worthy. . . ."

Unfortunately, the song is often delayed until after the presider, the concelebrants, the deacon, the servers, the readers, the eucharistic ministers and the musicians have received communion, thereby inadvertently focusing attention on the communion of the servants of the assembly rather than on the sharing in the eucharist by the entire assembly.

There are several ways to improve the flow of this section of the Mass. One suggestion is very simple. Make sure that the musicians realize that they are to begin the song while the presider is receiving communion. Then the priest distributes the body of the Lord to the eucharistic ministers, and they help distribute the blood of the Lord to each other before proceeding to their stations. Thus they are seen to affirm faith in "the body of Christ" before they ask others to affirm that same faith. One team of eucharistic ministers may be designated to make sure that the choir will receive communion and are not left out from sharing in the sacred banquet. Another solution is for the singers to join the communion procession after the song is underway, and to make sure that the instrumentalists receive when the song is over.

A second suggestion is based on the instruction to the deacon about consuming what remains of the precious blood after he administers the cup to the assembly (2000 GIRM, 182). In many churches, in order not to prolong the communion of the various liturgical ministers into a separate rite while the assembly waits for its communion in silence, the eucharistic ministers are the last of the assembly to receive communion. This can suggest to those present that these ministers are truly servants of the assembly, waiting until everyone else has been served before they themselves share in communion.

However, this practice should be choreographed carefully because it too can convey unintended meanings. For example, when all the eucharistic ministers line up behind the presider at the altar and eat the eucharistic bread simultaneously (in a way in which no one else has done), attention is focused on these ministers and an unintended sense of specialness, that is, a new clericalism, may be conveyed visually.

Perhaps a better approach is the one suggested by Gabe Huck in *The Communion Rite at Sunday Mass* (p. 80). The first team of eucharistic ministers to finish returns to the credence table and two of them station themselves there, one with a plate and the other with a cup. When other eucharistic ministers return, after setting down their cups and plates, they receive communion from the first team of ministers along with readers, servers and any singers or musicians near the sanctuary. The fact that these ministers receive communion last shows them to be servants of the assembly. The fact that they receive in a procession as all others have done shows that they are not given any special privilege or distinction.

Communion is a time of unity—with God and God's people. The assembly as a whole is nourished with the body and blood of Christ. Everything should be arranged to emphasize that unity, through song and through attention to all the details of how the assembly and its ministers receive communion together.

What is the proper posture for the assembly during and after communion?

The 2000 *General Instruction of the Roman Missal* addresses the posture of the assembly in paragraph 42, where it sees the "uniformity in posture" as a visible "sign of . . . the unity of the members of the Christian community." Paragraph 43 gives a few general guidelines as to when the assembly should assume which posture.

Upon examining these guidelines, the following basic rule can be detected: With two exceptions, the assembly assumes the same posture as the presiding priest. Thus, in general, when the priest is standing, so should everyone in the assembly. When the priest sits, so should everyone in the assembly.

The two exceptions are (1) during the preparation of the gifts, when the priest is standing and the assembly is seated, and (2) during the homily, when the assembly is seated but the priest is usually standing—although the *Introduction to the Lectionary* explicitly allows the priest to sit at the chair and preach the homily (#26). One should note that the U.S. practice of kneeling during the eucharistic prayer (after the Sanctus) is not prescribed in general by the GIRM, which sees standing as the general posture for the assembly during the entire eucharistic prayer and mentions kneeling only "at the consecration, except when prevented by reasons of health, lack of space, the large number of people present or some other good reason." The GIRM does say that the practice may be "laudably retained."

Regarding the communion rite, paragraph 43 of the GIRM states the following: "the faithful should stand . . . from the invitation *Pray, brethren* before the prayer over the gifts to the end of the Mass." Only two exceptions are mentioned: sitting, "as circumstances allow, during the period of sacred silence after communion," and, as just noted, kneeling at the consecration unless good reason suggests otherwise.

What the GIRM presents as normative practice is this: After the eucharistic prayer, the entire assembly should be standing throughout the Lord's Prayer, the sign of peace and the breaking of the bread accompanied by the *Agnus Dei*. They should continue to stand during the invitation to communion and the distribution of communion, as well as after communion, until the presiding priest returns to the chair and sits down to signal the beginning of the period of silent prayer.

The assumption of the 2000 GIRM is that as soon as the invitation to communion is finished and the priest receives communion, the communion song is begun without delay (#86 and 159). The entire assembly is assumed to be standing and joining in the song as they approach to receive communion, as they return to their places, and even after they return, until after the last person has received communion. Only then should the communion hymn cease and everyone sit in communal silent prayer.

The GIRM does not sanction the all-too-common practice of kneeling after the *Agnus Dei* for the invitation to communion, or of kneeling after returning from partaking in the eucharistic elements. Yet because kneeling at these moments has been common practice in many parts of the country, the U.S. bishops have permitted this practice to continue, but the diocesan bishop may make other determinations for his diocese.

As Saint Augustine said, the eucharist is the sign of unity. It seems odd, therefore, that at the great moment when the assembly partakes of the holy bread and sacred cup that makes them all one in Christ, so many people are visibly disunited in their posture—some standing, others kneeling, others sitting! Certainly, we need to reflect on our actions, especially on the meaning of our participation in the sacred meal in which we partake of the body and blood of Christ. But during this communal activity of worship, we also need to realize the importance of our visible solidarity with others through song and action. The proper moment for our individual thoughts and personal prayer to Christ, whose body and blood we have shared, is during the communal period of sacred silence after all have finished partaking in the eucharist.

What is the recent history of the laity serving as communion ministers? Have the rules been changed now?

Lately a few critics have said that the typical use of lay people as ministers of communion in parishes is an abuse. These critics invoke some relatively recent Vatican documents and claim that lay people are not needed in this ministry except under the most dire circumstances. Their claims range from simply denying that the typical number of people at Mass is too many for the priest alone (or the priest and deacon alone) to distribute communion, to arguing that lay people distributing communion is somehow less respectful or downright disrespectful to the blessed sacrament.

A pastor in Kentucky, for example, told a newspaper that he was dismissing the parish's communion ministers. They had done a good job, he noted. But using "extraordinary" ministers of communion on a regular, scheduled basis was contrary to the Vatican's wishes, he claimed. He said that the extra time it takes for him to distribute communion personally to every one (under one form, of course), is not bad—it slows the liturgy to a more reverent pace. And besides, he claims that by restricting the distribution of communion to himself he is better defining his ordained ministry vis-a-vis the laity. When asked about giving communion under both forms, this pastor explained that now he only does that when the assembly is small and the deacon is present.

At a parish in another state, the pastor recently told all priests on the staff to help in the distribution of communion at all Masses on Sundays, again citing the wishes of the Vatican. Older Catholics may remember the days before 1970 when most priests of the parish had to rush from the rectory at communion time at every Sunday Mass to help distribute the eucharist, lest the Mass be unreasonably lengthened. In parishes with numerous Masses, this meant that most of the priests were "on call" almost all Sunday morning, every Sunday. This practice was necessitated by the tradition then in effect that only an ordained deacon, priest or bishop could distribute communion.

It sometimes degenerated into the ridiculous: Public address speakers from the church were installed in the rectory living room or kitchen, where the priests not presiding at Mass sat around, sometimes vested, drinking coffee, smoking cigarettes and chatting, waiting for the beginning of the *Agnus Dei* to make their appearance.

Is the Vatican really asking for this to be restored? Is the Vatican asking for a change in practice?

In 1973 the Holy See issued the instruction, *Immensae caritatis* ("Of Immense Love" [DOL, 2073ff]), which regularized the permissions it had given privately since around 1969 to permit laypersons to distribute communion as "extraordinary" or "special" ministers of the eucharist. Individuals who received the "mandate" could exercise this ministry when the number of people wishing to receive communion would unduly prolong the Mass were the priest to distribute communion by himself (part 1, section Ic). The same document stated that priests should remember that the presence of extraordinary ministers did "not release them from the obligation of giving the eucharist to the faithful" (part 1, section VI).

The introduction of lay communion ministers was actually a return to a practice of the early church in which distributing the eucharist was not restricted to those who were ordained, but where households took the eucharist home with them after the Sunday celebration, and distributed it to each other, particularly to the sick, during the week.

Involving lay people in ministerial roles is proper by reason of their baptism and their God-given talents—not to mention the nature of the liturgy itself. At the same time, liturgical principles should not be ignored, and there is a tradition which states that the roles of each minister must be balanced with those of others and no one should usurp the proper functions of another (see 2000 GIRM, 91 and 99). It is proper to involve all present fully in the eucharistic action taking place (see *Constitution on the Liturgy,* 11 and 14), but this does not mean, of course, that every one in church has to have a role beyond that of participating as the assembly. Assuming that every one has to do every thing would actually hinder rather than help the celebration and is contrary to good liturgical principles! The liturgy works according to the Pauline image of the one body made up of many parts, with each part taking its proper role.

Because of certain "abuses" (we assume prompted by good intentions), the Holy See issued *Inaestimabile Donum* ("Priceless Gift") in 1980, a set of norms which attempted to respond to practices considered not in keeping with established regulations or liturgical tradition. This document reaffirmed the practice of having extraordinary ministers assist the priest in distributing communion at Mass, but also scolded priests who, "though present at the celebration, refrain from distributing communion and leave this task to the laity" (#10).

The question of whether it is permitted for extraordinary ministers of communion to exercise their ministry when there are enough priests and deacons present at a Mass was asked of the Pontifical Commission for the *Authentic Interpretation of the Code of Canon Law* after the promulgation of the 1983 code. In 1987 the Commission decided that this practice was, in fact, against the spirit of the original decree and the subsequent canons, since lay people distributing communion should be considered as a "suppletory ministry," that is, one which is exercised only when there are not enough "ordinary" ministers (that is, deacons, priests and bishops) for the occasion (see BCL Newsletter, vol. XXIV, February, 1988).

The actual text of the question is worthy of note since it reads, "when there are present in the church ordinary ministers, even if they are not participating in the eucharistic celebration." The phrasing of the question echoes the 1980 document in referring to those "present." Neither of these two documents refer to those deacons or priests who are not physically present within the church building!

The instruction issued by the Holy See in August 1997 regarding the collaboration of the laity with priests in various ministerial activities also addressed the topic of extraordinary ministers of the eucharist in article 8. (This is the document that most critics of lay people serving as communion ministers cite.) But this instruction did not change any law in this regard. It merely reiterated what had appeared earlier, emphasizing again that lay people may serve as eucharistic ministers "when there are no ordained ministers *present*" or when the ordained ministers "present at a liturgical celebration" are unable to help. There is no explicit mention of priests or deacons coming to the church solely to assist at communion time.

The noted American liturgist, the late Father Robert Hovda, in his book *Strong, Loving, and Wise,* pointed out that one thing the presiding priest *must* do at Mass is personally distribute the eucharist (pp. 36–37 [1980 printing]). Sharing the eucharistic meal with the assembly is a core activity related to presiding at the eucharist and, as such, it should be considered a privileged ministerial moment cherished by all those ordained to serve God's people. This is a good principle: It would be strange for the presider to sit down while others distributed communion.

But insisting that the presider participate in the distribution of communion is not the same thing as insisting that *only* the presider do so, or that *only* ordained ministers be allowed to do so. Liturgical law clearly allows otherwise.

The rubrics tacitly assume that all the ministers who function at Mass have been present throughout. Nowhere is the custom of a preacher coming in from the sacristy merely for the homily ever mentioned, nor the older custom of priests helping out solely during the distribution of communion. In fact, the opposite is true: The GIRM prohibits priests who may be late from joining in a concelebration (2000 GIRM, 206). It also seems liturgically inauthentic and inconsistent for someone to distribute communion within Mass and not receive communion him- or herself! (We would *never* allow extraordinary ministers of communion to do this.)

Canonical tradition cautions against establishing practices that go beyond or are even contrary to explicit norms. For example, since no Roman document ever explicitly permits the distribution of the reserved eucharist in the tabernacle at Mass and the contrary is actually very strongly encouraged (2000 GIRM, 85), one goes against liturgical norms when there is no real need and one uses hosts in the tabernacle at Mass either exclusively or as a regular practice (even though this, unfortunately, is an all-too-common occurrence).

In a similar fashion, since there is no explicit permission for priests who have not been physically present for the eucharist to function in a significant role merely for a few minutes, and the documents specifically mention priests "present" in the church, one is hard-pressed to justify (see 2000 GIRM, 162) requiring priests to come from a rectory solely to distribute communion for a few minutes and then leave.

This issue is probably not of major urgency in most parishes of the United States, given that many parishes have only one resident priest and some parishes have none. Churches in the United States often have several hundred people present at Mass on Sunday and communion is distributed under both kinds. Extraordinary ministers are of necessity. But in some European countries, there may be several priests present in a larger cathedral and relatively few people present for a Mass. In such cases there may be no need for lay communion ministers.

This issue also raises the question of how one should interpret liturgical laws so that the best of liturgical tradition is preserved, and so that we do not read more into a law than the law is meant to require. Given the declining numbers of active priests, the increasing median age, and the greater demands placed on priests in most parishes, parish priests need to understand their physical limits and not burden themselves to the possible detriment of their overall ministerial effectiveness and physical health. It certainly is a wonderful statement of solidarity and of priestly devotion when many of the clergy of a parish are seen by parishioners each Sunday, either functioning throughout the whole course of the eucharistic celebration or greeting parishioners before or after the liturgy. Yet increasing visibility at the expense of authentic liturgical practices, as when priests appear only for distributing communion, seems far less than the ideal of liturgy envisioned by the revised liturgical books.

At a Mass in a parish I visited recently, after the formal invitation to communion, the priest announced that everyone was welcome to join in the communion procession to the altar, and that those who were not Catholic or did not wish to receive communion should hold their right hand on their chest as a sign that they wished to receive a blessing instead. What is the status of this practice?

As many people have come to realize since the implementation of the RCIA, the presence of non-communicants during the liturgy of the eucharist is a theological anomaly — even if common. The ancient practice, re-introduced in Catholic worship with the RCIA, was that catechumens were dismissed after the liturgy of the word and only those who could partake of the eucharistic elements remained for the rest of the celebration. Ancient tradition also permitted baptized infants to receive communion, a tradition still observed by many Eastern churches. Hence, in such a situation there was no one present who was not able to partake of the eucharistic elements.

The situation common in most Roman rite parishes today, however, is far different from that of the early church. Small children are present who have not "made their first communion." Non-Catholic spouses are present with their families. Catholics conscious of serious sin usually do not partake of the eucharist before celebrating reconciliation. Hence, it is common that a significant number of people present for the eucharist not to be able to receive communion.

In various places recently, in order to be hospitable and to avoid making people feel ignored, self-conscious, or stigmatized by remaining in a pew by themselves during communion, celebrants have invited all present to participate in the communion procession while also inviting non-Catholics to request a blessing instead of partaking of the eucharistic bread and wine.

In fact, in his encyclical, *Ut Unum Sint,* Pope John Paul II refers to special ecumenical occasions when he participated in this ritual and himself blessed non-communicants who approached him in the communion procession (#72). Hence this practice has been given a kind of approval because of papal precedent, yet there is no document that explicitly encourages or permits its use.

Non-communicants have been participating in the communion procession for centuries whenever parents carry an infant or lead a pre-schooler by the hand with them as the parents receive communion. The novelty in the contemporary practice is the explicit acknowledgement of the presence of non-communicants by means of a blessing while the eucharistic elements are being shared with communicants.

Using one procession for "double duty" is something that generally should be avoided since it confuses the meaning of the action. For example, on Ash Wednesday, we should never combine distributing ashes with sharing communion. On Good Friday, we should never combine venerating the cross with sharing communion. Each activity is important enough for its own presentation.

Yet, perhaps this modern practice is in some way different since it does really focus on "communion." Whether one receives the eucharistic elements and expresses communion with the church or whether one receives a blessing indicating that one is not in communion or that one has somehow damaged his or her communion with the church, in either case, one says something about ecclesial and eucharistic communion in our modern world, and the painful divisions among Christians which inhibit ecclesial communion and thus prohibit eucharistic communion.

As a practical matter, many older churches were built during a time when few people went to communion at Mass and the spacing between pews did not easily permit people to pass by others who choose to remain in their places. As a result, it can be distracting and even hazardous for a few people to remain in place in a pew while the majority are forced to move past them (often very awkwardly) during this central moment of the liturgy.

I have mixed feeling about this contemporary practice. On the one hand, I dislike seeing family units broken up in churches, when a non-Catholic parent must stay in the pew while the Catholic parent comes with the children to receive the eucharist. The pain of division is felt enough in homes and we should do whatever is possible to avoid exacerbating such divisions while celebrating the sacrament of unity. On the other hand, there is something less than ideal when individuals come up together in one liturgical action for two different purposes.

I suggest at this point of our history, we should avoid making rash judgments about the merits or problems of this practice, and reflect on it a bit more. The Lord is calling us all to share in the one bread and the one cup. It may be a while before we are able to assimilate all the pros and cons, and, with the assistance of the Divine Spirit, be able to judge whether this practice is an aid or a hindrance in achieving that ultimate unity Christ so intensely prayed for before he died!

Concluding Rites

Should the Book of the Gospels or the lectionary be carried out at the end of the liturgy? Some say no, because the readings have been proclaimed and the book should remain in the sanctuary. Others say yes, suggesting that we go forth to proclaim God's word. What do you think?

Neither the 2000 *General Instruction of the Roman Missal* nor the *Ceremonial of Bishops* offers much guidance on the procession at the end of Mass or of any other liturgy. This, of itself, suggests some restraint concerning certain aspects of this practical, and rather anticlimactic, ritual action. Most of the time, the sole purpose of the final procession is to get the ministers out of the church in an orderly fashion.

In describing the basic form of celebrating Mass, paragraph 169 of the 2000 GIRM summarizes the final procession by merely saying that after kissing the altar and making a profound bow, the priest "leaves." The rubric for a Mass with a deacon, 2000 GIRM, 186, states that the deacon "leaves in the manner followed for the entrance procession" (2000 GIRM, 186). There is no mention of any sort of recessional hymn, nor any mention of items carried, such as cross, candles, incense or the like. (Even paragraph 170 of the *Ceremonial of Bishops* adds only that those in the final procession should follow "the order in which they entered.")

The only times the liturgical books give more details about a final procession are when they describe the procession to the grave after a funeral Mass, the procession with the oils after the Chrism Mass, and the procession with the blessed sacrament after the Mass of the Lord's Supper (Holy Thursday) or on the solemnity of the Body and Blood of Christ.

We should also note that the 2000 GIRM and CB specify that the Book of the Gospels is to be carried in the entrance procession rather than the lectionary (2000 GIRM, 120d; CB, 128), which is presumed to be already at the ambo (2000 GIRM, 118b; CB, 125). There is a long tradition, especially in the East, that the Book of the Gospels is a special icon of Christ's presence and is particularly appropriate to be carried (as the cross is at any procession, or the paschal candle is at the Easter Vigil) when a passage from the gospel will be subsequently proclaimed. As such, it is symbolic but also functional: Liturgical authenticity would suggest that the Book of the Gospels should not be carried into the assembly if the gospel will not actually be read from that book!

Our contemporary sensitivity to the holiness of all of scripture has raised questions about separating the gospels from the rest of the lectionary, except when specifically demanded by tradition, such as at the ordination of deacons and bishops. And so, particularly in the United States, it has been common for the lectionary to be carried in the entrance procession in place of the Book of the Gospels. Yet none of these concerns or customs particularly addresses the use of a book of scripture in the final procession.

The lack of details in the Roman liturgical books about the final procession suggests that restraint is appropriate. There is always the danger of emphasizing what is minor and downplaying what should be of greater importance. It is always appropriate to lead any procession with the processional cross between two candles as a way of proclaiming that we should glory in the cross of our Lord (see Galatians 6:14) and proclaim Christ crucified (see 1 Corinthians 1:23). Hence, if the cross leads the ministers into the church, it may be used (but is not necessary) to lead them out at the end.

The final procession is mainly functional. It is an organized, dignified way to have the ministers leave the assembly and, in a sense, lead the rest of the assembly into the world from which they came. Thus, in general, items not needed (such as incense) would not be carried (unless the item was just used, such as incense at a funeral, or would be needed for a rite to follow).

Some authors have suggested that even though it is appropriate to honor the Book of the Gospels solemnly by carrying it in procession while the Alleluia is sung and lifting it high before the gospel proclamation, it is not appropriate to raise the lectionary or the Book of the Gospels after the proclamation of the scripture passage. That can draw focus toward the object of the book to the detriment of the active word that should be received in the hearts of all in the assembly. The same line of reasoning would suggest that even though the books of scripture should be treated with reverence, the word of God takes on a new dimension, as do the eucharistic elements, after the word has been heard and the eucharist has been received by members of the assembly. The word of God and the body of Christ can be seen as being taken from the church interiorly by each member of the assembly after the liturgy.

Considering these and other concerns, I think that in general it probably would be better to leave the lectionary and Book of the Gospels in an appropriate place near the ambo rather than carry either out during the final procession.

What are the rules regarding the recessional hymn at Mass?

There is no mention anywhere in the 2000 *General Instruction of the Roman Missal* of the common practice of singing a hymn at the end of Mass. In fact, the only mention in the GIRM of any sort of "procession" at the end of Mass occurs in the sections dealing with the deacon (#186) and with the acolyte (#193). Elsewhere, the GIRM or the rubrics of the *Order of Mass* merely say that the priest "leaves" after the blessing and dismissal (see, for example, #169), and does not mention a formal procession or any sort of hymn.

The *Ceremonial of Bishops* clarifies the lack of guidance slightly when it states that at a stational Mass, the ministers return to the sacristy "in procession, following the order in which they entered" (#170). But there is no mention of "recessional hymn."

There seem to be only three instances in which a formal hymn is prescribed for what may be called a "recessional," and in each of them the concluding procession is special because something is being carried as part of this procession. At the Chrism Mass, the hymn "O Redeemer" is prescribed as the recessional hymn to accompany the carrying of the holy oils out of the body of the church and into the sacristy. At the Mass of the Lord's Supper or Holy Thursday, the hymn "Sing, My Tongue" is prescribed as the recessional hymn to accompany the carrying of the blessed sacrament to the chapel of reservation. And at a funeral Mass, the hymn "May the Angels Lead You into Paradise" is given as one option to accompany the carrying of the body of the deceased from the church to the cemetery.

It does seem odd that such a common practice as a recessional hymn has no basis in any liturgical book. The document *Music in Catholic Worship* acknowledges the practice of using a recessional song (#73), but comments that it "has never been an official part of the rite." All this suggests that perhaps communities need to rethink local practice regarding the type of hymns sung at the end of Mass and whether one should be sung at all!

The last hymn mentioned in the GIRM is the hymn of praise that concludes the period of silent prayer after communion (#88 and 164). Some communities have successfully introduced a rousing hymn at this point in the liturgy and have made this the last hymn of the Mass. After a few moments of total silence after communion (complete silence, without any parish announcements—which are supposed to come *after* the prayer after communion), the assembly is invited to stand, and all praise God through a communal hymn. Then, after the prayer after communion, any brief announcements, the blessing, and the dismissal, instrumental music accompanies the procession of ministers as they leave the sanctuary and go to the doors of the church.

People have pointed out in various writings that it seems odd to have the deacon or priest formally dismiss the assembly only to have the cantor (in effect) tell them to ignore the dismissal and stay to sing one last song. In a sense, for the assembly to witness to the liturgical truth of the diaconal invitation to "go in peace," they should rightly leave, and even join the ministers in leaving, the church building.

Old customs are difficult to change, and people may be attached to even relatively recent customs. Many places seem "wedded" to rousing recessionals or to "meditation" hymns after communion sung by soloists or by the choir. But it is interesting to note that none of these practices is justified by the GIRM. It does not mention any recessional; when it does mention a hymn after communion, it explicitly states that it should be "sung by the entire congregation" (#88); and the posture of the assembly during the singing should be standing (see #43).

It might be good for parish liturgy committees to reflect on parish practice with regard to final hymns (after communion and as a "recessional") and to consider whether a change in practice could actually lead to better liturgy. On those occasions when a communal hymn is judged to be appropriate, it should reflect the liturgical season, the occasion or the action taking place ("sending-forth"), or it should be a generic hymn of thanks or praise (such as "Now Thank We All Our God").

Ministers

What are the proper liturgical roles for a deacon?

By a tradition based on the Acts of the Apostles, the deacon is seen as the servant of the community, and this role as servant is the foundation for determining the various diaconal activities during a liturgy. As servant, the deacon is the chief assistant to the presiding bishop or priest at a liturgy and also the main servant of the assembly gathered. His role is to facilitate the assembly's worship but not lead it himself. The 2000 *General Instruction of the Roman Missal* outlines in detail the specifics of the deacon's duties during Mass (#171–186). They may be summarized as follows.

The spoken texts associated with a deacon include the proclamation of the gospel, the litanies (the Lord, have mercy and the general intercessions) and the directions to the assembly. Some examples of such directions are as follows: "Let us offer each other a sign of peace," "Let us kneel," "Bow your heads and pray for God's blessing" and "Go in peace." During the Easter Vigil, it is the deacon's duty to proclaim Christ's resurrection by singing the *Exsultet* (if he is able to sing well).

The ritual activities associated with a deacon include caring for the Book of the Gospels and for the cup. The care for the book is shown by the deacon carrying it with reverence during the entrance and gospel processions. The care for the cup is shown by the deacon pouring the wine and water into it, while saying the proper prayer, during the preparation of the gifts; by elevating the cup at the end of the eucharistic prayer, and by ministering communion at the assembly from the cup (and consuming what remains after communion).

The deacon is the one to worry about the details of the worship taking place (if his training prepares him to do this). He functions as a "right hand man" for a bishop, and two deacons normally should assist as "chaplains" to a bishop rather than two priests. (See paragraph 26 of the *Ceremonial of Bishops*.)

While assisting at the liturgy, the deacon does not usurp the role of the presider (and concelebrating priests should not usurp the duties of a deacon). In fact, traditionally, the deacon never says any presidential prayers and does not make use of presidential gestures. For example, the deacon keeps his hands joined while greeting the assembly before the gospel (2000 GIRM, 175) and whenever giving directions to the assembly.

At noneucharistic celebrations, the deacon's functions are similar to what occur during Mass if he assists someone else presiding. If, however, because of the absence of a bishop or priest a deacon presides at a baptism, wedding, funeral or blessing, he uses the same gestures and texts as a priest. Deacons, however, should be mindful that their role as presider in these special cases is an innovation because of pastoral necessity. Thus, what is appropriate for deacons to do in the absence of a priest is not necessarily appropriate when priests are present.

Deacons are ordained ministers whose primary liturgical role is that of service. In this ministry, the deacon thus becomes a vivid icon of Christ, "who came not to be served, but to serve."

What are the major qualifications and responsibilities of altar servers?

The duties of the servers have evolved over the years. Before 1963 their primary duties were to pronounce the memorized Latin responses and to assist the priest by moving the missal, ringing the sanctuary bells, and bringing water and wine to the altar. The servers were the only people permitted in the sanctuary other than priests.

In contemporary liturgical celebrations, there are several kinds of ministers that serve the assembly; no longer is a server or other minister defined as one who "helps Father." All who have a leadership role in the liturgical action are true "servers" of the assembly, but before they are servers, they are members. For example, they should be attentive to whomever is speaking, and join in communal activities such as singing and responding. They are, in a sense, role models for the rest of the assembly.

As people with particular roles in the liturgy, they should possess adequate skills for their ministries. Readers must be able to read well. Servers should be strong enough to hold the sacramentary, and old enough to exhibit an appropriate "presence" before a large gathering.

The 2000 *General Instruction of the Roman Missal* mentions the specific duties of altar servers (#187–193), although this section technically refers to those who have been officially instituted in the ministry of acolyte. Servers carry the censer, incense, cross and candles in processions. They hold the sacramentary for the presider during the opening and concluding rites, bring the cloths, vessels and sacramentary for the liturgy of the eucharist to and from the altar, and help with the bread, wine, water and handwashing as needed. Those who can perform these tasks with decorum, in addition to their tasks as assembly members, are qualified to be altar servers.

Where should the servers sit during the liturgy?

During the decade immediately following Vatican II, sanctuary furniture was sometimes rearranged too quickly and without sufficient reflection on the implications. In some places the three-seat sedilia was merely reoriented. Rather than facing the opposite wall of the sanctuary while seated, the priest and the two servers on either side of him now faced the rest of the assembly. Little thought was given to the appropriateness of seating secondary ministers in such a prominent location.

The pre-Vatican II sedilia was a concession to human weakness—it was a place out of direct view of the assembly for the priest, with the deacon and the subdeacon or with two servers, to rest during the singing of the Gloria and the Credo or while another cleric was preaching the sermon. It was not in itself a locus for liturgical action, since almost all of the liturgy took place at the altar. The missal of Paul VI reestablished the presidential chair as a place at which the presiding priest normally leads certain sections of liturgies—it no longer is merely a place where the priest and his assistants sit when tired or when someone else is doing something.

Given the symbolic nature of the chair and the role of the priest who uses it, care should be taken lest the power of this liturgical symbol be unknowingly diluted.

The *2000 General Instruction of the Roman Missal* mentions that the deacon sits next to the priest at the chair (# 174 and 310). But when the GIRM refers to places for acolytes and other ministers, it says that their seats should be in the sanctuary (#188), distinguished from those for the clergy while remaining convenient so that the ministers can carry out their duties (#189 and 310).

Similar instructions are found in the *Ceremonial of Bishops.* It mentions that two deacons stand on either side of the bishop at the cathedra at the cathedral (#131). But it also suggests that seats be provided in the sanctuary for other ministers of the liturgy (#50) and that other deacons and ministers should be seated apart from any concelebrating priests (#136).

Careful reflection on these texts and on the symbolic nature of the liturgy suggests that the place where ministers are seated can be significant. Just as where someone sits at the family dinner table suggests that person's role in the family, so also at the eucharistic banquet. There is only one president of the assembly who serves by leading the assembly in prayer. He is assisted by the deacon, who at the eucharist proclaims the gospel and cares for the cup. Because of their unified roles as leaders of prayer throughout the liturgy, these two individuals are appropriately seated at a special place, visible to all present, to enable them to exercise their presidential and diaconal roles.

Other individuals either exercise their ministry for the community at one particular point in the liturgy (as do readers and eucharistic ministers) or assist the priest and deacon as needed (by holding the book or bringing vessels to the altar). Hence, it follows that these other ministers should be seated away from the presidential chair yet close enough so that they can discreetly and gracefully move to exercise their individual ministries at the chair, ambo or altar.

This same principle even applies to the positioning of concelebrating priests. Although ancient Roman documents suggest that concelebrants were commonly seated in the apse surrounding the presiding bishop, a similar arrangement in modern churches could give a confused image. When concelebrants are seated in a single line all facing the assembly and are vested identically, one gets the image of a committee leading the liturgy rather than of the presidency of one person joined in a special way by fellow priests. One occasionally sees a principal celebrant being assisted by two "chief" concelebrants who help at the chair and the altar. Such a practice incorrectly mimics the roles of the deacon and subdeacon at the Tridentine Solemn Mass and is contrary to good contemporary liturgical practices.

Leadership in the Christian community is leadership imitating Jesus, who came not to be served but to serve (Mark 10:45).

The presidency of the presiding priest at the liturgy is one of service to the assembly by vocalizing the prayer of the community before God and coordinating the tasks of other ministers. It is not a leadership of domination or autocracy, and thus it is not a leadership that should in any way be diluted.

This does not mean that the presidential chair should be distant from the rest of the assembly! The seating in some churches is so arranged that the place for the presider is visually and physically part of the seating of the assembly yet is a place from which the presider can lead the assembly in prayer.

All ministers other than the presider—deacons, servers, readers, eucharistic ministers, concelebrating priests, ushers, cantors, musicians—are part of the assembly that is being led in prayer by the presiding priest. Yet they assist the presiding priest in serving the body of Christ. Where they sit should respect both the unique role of the presiding priest as well as their own special functions as servants to the assembled people of God.

Can communion ministers still help consume the remaining precious blood after the distribution of communion and cleanse the vessels? I've seen reports in papers that seem to indicate a change in this practice with the publication of the new GIRM.

Some of the changes in the 2000 GIRM may need clarification in the months and years ahead, especially given certain well-established pastoral practices in some countries. Sometimes the first answer proposed, especially in the press, may not be nuanced enough, may not have taken into account all the canonical legislation on the matter, and may need to be rethought in terms of other considerations.

One should first note that there has been only a minor change in the text of the GIRM regarding who can cleanse the vessels. Between paragraph 238 of the 1975 GIRM and paragraph 279 of the 2000 GIRM, the only change was the addition of the adjective "instituted" before "acolyte." The text now reads thus: "The vessels are cleansed by the priest or by the deacon or an instituted acolyte after communion or after Mass, if possible at a side table." This addition of "instituted" merely clarifies the meaning of "acolyte" rather than makes any substantial changes. The 1975 GIRM only mentioned "extraordinary minister" in relation to an acolyte (1975 GIRM, 65). The 2000 GIRM mentions extraordinary ministers in several places but the underlying presupposition is that priests and deacons are the normal ministers at communion. Thus one should not jump to any conclusion that the omission of the explicit mention of "extraordinary ministers" in the list of those who can cleanse the vessels should be seen as a prohibition of this practice. The 2000 GIRM does not prohibit this practice any more than the 1975 GIRM did! And, in fact, when a clarification was requested regarding whether other ministers could help cleanse the vessels, a reply was given in 1978 that "the remarks on the priest, deacon, and acolyte are applicable to an extraordinary minister" (*Notitiae,* 14 [1978] pp. 593–594 [DOL 1628 footnote R42]).

One should also note that the rite of administering communion to the sick by an extraordinary minister explicitly states that if such a minister distributes the precious blood, that minister must consume what remains and then wash the vessels (*Holy Communion and Worship of the Eucharist Outside of Mass,* 55).

Paragraph 107 of the 2000 GIRM expands on paragraph 70 of the former GIRM in mentioning that certain liturgical offices (including that of acolyte) may be committed to laity. Those who are given any such liturgical office are entrusted with all the duties associated with the office. There is no explicit mention of cleansing vessels being "reserved" to the priest and deacon as the 2000 GIRM does about the breaking of the bread (#83).

Once again, some clarification may be needed about such practices, but until that time, there seems to be no need to change established practice. Who cleanses the vessels, in perspective, is really a secondary issue in comparison to many other liturgical questions for the church of the twenty-first century!

Weekdays

Presiding at daily Mass, I usually have no lector or servers and sometimes only a total of ten people. Is it all right to do the greetings, orations and readings from the altar? The chair is too far away and the ambo seems too formal for such a small assembly. Using the altar, I can set everything there before Mass and I don't feel foolish walking around the sanctuary.

The rites and rubrics in most post-Vatican II liturgical books assume a good-sized assembly that includes a full complement of ministers. One of the major challenges in the on-going process of liturgical renewal is to accommodate our rites appropriately when the actual situation is significantly different from the norm envisioned in the books.

A few of the documents offer some guidance and direction: *The Directory for Masses with Children* offers general guidelines for certain adaptations; the U.S. Bishops' document *Music in Catholic Worship* takes care to point out which parts of the liturgy are primary and which are secondary; and the notes in *Pastoral Care of the Sick* speak about involving people in the celebration even when very few are present.

One sees a whole range of practices during weekday liturgies. Some places have a well-arranged chapel appropriate for a group of thirty or less and use it regularly for most weekday Masses. Other places always use the main church, even if it seats over a thousand. Some parishes include singing, accompanied by an organist, at the most attended weekday Masses; others sing only the Alleluia and Amen, and others have no singing at all. In some places, the priest proclaims all the readings, while in other places readers and eucharistic ministers are regularly present for all weekday Masses.

When the assembly comprises very few people and there are no ministers other than the presider, some priests tend to use the "choreography" described in pragraphs 252 through 272 of the 2000 *General Instruction of the Roman Missal* for a Mass at which only one minister assists. In a sense this mimics the rubrics of the Tridentine Missal, which prescribed that everything was done at the altar by the priest alone, with the servers offering the responses. Note, however, that even in this case, the GIRM says the readings should be proclaimed from the ambo or a lectern (#260).

To do everything at the altar when a congregation is present—even only a few people—is unfortunate for several reasons. The liturgy is "the work of the people"—the whole people—and actions that invite or encourage the assembly to be passive observers instead of active participants are best avoided. It may be helpful to see a small assembly as a positive pastoral opportunity rather than as a negative burden. Pastoral practices that are good for people's faith but impractical in a large Sunday assembly often can be employed when an assembly is small.

For example, it is relatively easy for a group of twenty or so to move in procession from one location (where the liturgy of the word might be celebrated) to another (for example, to surround the altar for the liturgy of the eucharist). This may never be possible on Sunday if the assembly is large and the room not large enough. Small assemblies provide tremendous opportunities to make fuller use of liturgical movement and space than would be possible with a typical Sunday assembly.

It might be possible for a priest to lead the introductory rite while standing near the people, perhaps in the main aisle of the church. The readings might then be proclaimed from a place next to the first pew, using a portable lectern, if necessary, or simply by having the reader hold the lectionary. The priest could sit near the people; perhaps the presider's chair could be moved closer to where the assembly sits for the week and then returned to its regular place for Sunday. At the procession with the gifts, the priest could move to the altar (perhaps accompanied by the whole assembly). In all of this, the priest is able to be physically close to the people in a way that may not be possible on Sundays. Leading all parts of the liturgy from the altar ignores the movement from the word to the eucharist.

One of the major results of the *Constitution on the Sacred Liturgy* was a renewed sense of a distribution of roles. For example, priests should not perform the tasks proper to deacons or readers, and choirs should not usurp the role of the assembly. Allied to this is a renewed sense of liturgical space and an appreciation of ritual structure. The altar is for the bread and wine of Christ's body — only what is absolutely necessary should be placed on it (see 2000 GIRM, 306). And the ambo is for the book of God's holy Word — it should be used for proclaiming God's word alone (see 2000 GIRM, 309). We do damage to the symbolic nature of liturgy when we continue to ignore these often-overlooked distinctions.

For a priest to do everything at one place may also suggest that what is really important is the mere recitation of words, and that the symbolic nature of gesture and place can be ignored. We too often overlook the symbolic confusion that occurs when the cup and plate are set on the altar before Mass begins or when the cruets and the bowl for washing hands are left on the altar throughout the liturgy and not placed on a credence table. The altar is for the bread and wine of Christ's body and blood — the more that other items (including candles, microphones, cruets, eyeglasses and missalettes) clutter the altar, the less prominent the bread and wine become.

In addition, for a priest always to stand at the altar and, thus, always to have something between him and others in the assembly may present yet other undesirable non-verbal signals. Like the executive or principal who always sits or stands behind a desk, a priest standing behind an altar may signal to others that he needs a barrier to separate him from others.

Rather than making convenience the guiding rule for adaptations in small, weekday liturgies, a better approach might be to look to the principles underlying the rubrics and to see how they can be embodied in the given circumstance. Long-term solutions may be necessary: Some parishes have profitably adapted side chapels (or rectory or convent oratories) to make an appropriate worship space for weekday liturgies and still retain separate places for the presider, the word and the eucharist. Other places make use of an alternate ambo and presidential chair in the main body of the church that is more appropriately located for the numbers present on weekdays. Some places make use of movement and gesture not possible on Sundays. Other places have trained volunteers to function as weekday readers, servers, and eucharistic ministers. The story is told of one newly appointed pastor who bluntly challenged the weekday assembly. He said that he would faithfully do his part, but only his part: If people did not come forward to serve as readers, he would no longer read the first reading. It was a gamble, but it worked. A few people volunteered to take turns reading.

When a dozen people are present at a 6:30 AM weekday Mass, don't pretend that this is Christmas Midnight Mass. Yet don't assume that to accommodate the circumstances you have to ignore liturgy's nature. With some thought, planning, and care, it is possible to be faithful to fundamental liturgical principles while adapting to the worship space and savoring the peacefulness and intimacy that is frequently a hallmark of small, weekday liturgies.

Last year, we had two priests in our parish and two daily Masses—both in the morning, both attended by fifteen to thirty people. Now that one priest has been assigned elsewhere, should we schedule a communion service (to be led by the deacon) to replace the second daily Mass? If not, why not? And what should we do with the group of people that usually attends the discontinued Mass?

An ancient tradition of the church prescribed that the eucharist should only be celebrated once on any day in any church ("one church, one altar, one eucharist"). This rule is essentially still retained in the Roman rite during the Easter Triduum, when Masses at which only one minister assists are forbidden, a second liturgy is permitted only in special circumstances, and the distribution of communion outside of the liturgical services is prohibited (except to the sick or as viaticum).

In Orthodox churches, there is usually only one eucharist celebrated on Sundays. If a parish has several resident priests, typically they concelebrate at the single liturgy. Another priest may celebrate a second liturgy, but it usually takes place at a side chapel.

Before Vatican II, it was commonly expected that every priest would want to celebrate Mass every day. This fact, coupled with the prohibition against concelebration in the Roman rite, meant that in parishes where there were several priests, several Masses were scheduled and other priests celebrated Masses in convent chapels or at a side altar. The practice of multiple weekday Masses is still common in larger parishes and is something many older Catholics expect at their local parish church. But we need to realize that this practice is far from ancient and not really ideal.

The eucharist is the sacrament of unity—between individuals and with our God. The greatest sign of unity is when all members of a community gather together for a common meal—whether it be the community of a family at a wedding or the community of Christians at the eucharist. Thus every effort should be made to encourage common eucharistic celebrations whenever possible. Fewer celebrations are less likely to splinter the resources of the community as well, ensuring the presence of readers and eucharistic ministers and, on weekdays, possibly gathering enough people to facilitate singing.

When the retirement or reassignment of parish priests necessitates adjustments in the parish worship schedule, some thought should be given to reducing the number of Masses so as to encourage community unity. To minimize inconvenience to all, a neutral time might be chosen: If the Masses were at 7:00 AM and 9:00 AM, change the time to 8:00 AM. Or the time of Mass might be rotated, for example, 6:30 AM on Tuesday and Thursday, 8:00 AM on Monday, Wednesday and Friday. Neighboring parishes might also wish to coordinate times of weekday Masses for the convenience of all in the area. On major feasts, the bishop might permit priests to celebrate a second weekday Mass in the evening to encourage attendance.

Some parishes have profitably introduced the celebration of Morning Prayer before the first morning Mass, and this official daily prayer of the church might be accepted by some people as a liturgy in its own right on those days Mass is not celebrated.

For many reasons, introducing a communion service on weekdays when Mass is celebrated in the same church at a different time is not ideal. One major difficulty is that communion services continue to perpetuate the notion that the eucharist is primarily the consecrated elements stored in the tabernacle, more than, or rather than, the dynamic celebration of thanksgiving by the assembled community. Older parishioners may remember parishes where communion was regularly distributed immediately before and after

Mass as well as during Mass. The revised Roman rite, while permitting the distribution of communion outside Mass, encourages people to receive it during the celebration of the eucharist (see *Holy Communion and Worship of the Eucharist Outside of Mass,* 14).

We should make every effort to include those who cannot be present at parish Masses, such as the elderly and the infirm, by bringing the eucharist to them in their homes. But we should not make "convenience" an absolute good in itself. Given the resources of the parish and the nature of the eucharist as a celebration of unity, as a norm, one Mass on weekdays that is well celebrated and well attended would be preferable to several Masses or a combination of Masses and communion services.

On weekdays, to save on heating and cooling costs in our large church, we usually celebrate Mass in a small multi-purpose room in the parish center for the two dozen or so people who participate. Using a lectern, credence table and presidential chair in such a small setting seems unnecessary, so I lead the opening rites at the altar and the readers proclaim the readings from their places. I also leave the chalice and cruets on the altar throughout the Mass. Some members of the parish liturgy committee have suggested that I should change my practices. Any comments?

The 2000 *General Instruction of the Roman Missal* identifies four places where the liturgical actions of the Mass occur: the seats of the assembly (#311), the chair of the presider (#310), the ambo of God's word (#309) and the table of Christ's eucharist (#296). It also highlights the ancient tradition of the unique status of the altar as the table of the Lord's body and blood, noting that the Book of Gospels, the cup with the wine, the plate with the bread and the sacramentary are the only items that should be on the altar for any length of time (#306).

The space in which Mass is actually celebrated (whether in a small chapel in a large church or in a place not intended as a regular place of worship, such as a multi-purpose room) often conflicts with this renewed vision of the appropriate setting for the celebration of the Mass, as well as the appropriate reverence for the Lord's table. At times, local practices, such as using the altar as a credence table and ambo, also conflict with the vision found in the GIRM.

As a general rule, every attempt should be made to arrange places used for the celebration of liturgical rites according to the vision of the revised liturgical books. Nevertheless, one always needs to accommodate the demands of the actual community gathered in prayer. This is true whether the space is a centuries-old cathedral or a parish multi-purpose room, or whether the day is Easter Sunday or a weekday in Ordinary Time. Convenience should never be the primary guiding factor in determining how the liturgy is celebrated, and it should never outweigh fundamental liturgical principles.

The following are a few guidelines related to some common practices. There should always be a presider's chair from which the priest can lead the assembly in prayer. In smaller settings, the presidential chair can be placed near the ambo. Wherever it is located, the presider should be able to see the majority of those present and so easily lead the community in prayer from this place. In fidelity to the norms given in paragraph 124 of the GIRM, the opening rite should always be led from the chair, never from the altar.

Also, in fidelity to the GIRM (see #58, 260 and 309), the readings should be proclaimed from a fixed ambo, which is ideally at a significant distance from the altar. In smaller settings, it might be appropriate to have the altar and ambo face each other, with seats for the assembly on either side of these two liturgical focal points. In this way, the people face each other as well as altar and ambo. (This is called antiphonal or choir-style seating.) An old tradition sees the ambo primarily as a place rather than a piece of furniture, so if an adequate reading stand is unavailable, it is still important for the sake of maintaining the liturgical symbol to reserve one special place apart from the altar from which every proclamation of God's word takes place.

The homily may be preached by the presider from the presidential chair (2000 GIRM, 136; *Introduction to the Lectionary,* 26). This is especially appropriate at smaller liturgies.

Except for the altar cloth, the altar is ideally bare. Even candles are more appropriately placed around—rather than on— the altar (2000 GIRM, 307). There need not be a cross on the altar itself, since the priest is no longer required to look at a cross while at the altar. There should be a cross visible to the assembly, however, which can be mounted on the wall behind the altar; the processional cross placed in its stand also fulfills this requirement (2000 GIRM, 122 and 308).

Cruets should never be placed on the altar but on the credence table, where the chalice may also be prepared (see 2000 GIRM, 178). The chalice is normally left at the credence table until after the general intercessions.

When eucharist is celebrated with a small group in a small room, there is a natural inclination to be less formal than at a liturgy in a large church on a major feast. This is in conformity with the principles of the GIRM. But "less formal" and "more familiar" does not mean abandoning the basic principles of the Roman liturgy or dispensing with the fundamental nature of any liturgical rite as ritual, whether in text, gesture or posture. The ongoing challenge for any community, but particularly for presiders, is to celebrate with "full, conscious and active participation" by all, and to be faithful to the principles of the Roman liturgy while accommodating the people celebrating and the place of celebration. This is no small challenge!

Miscellaneous

A recent church goods catalogue advertised paper purificators. This seems like a good solution for us since our parish shares in communion from the cup at all Masses, and it seems that most of our cloth purificators are always at the laundry. Could you offer some guidance on this practice?

It would be simple to give a "yes" or "no" answer, but the use of paper napkins as purificators raises a more fundamental concern: Should efficiency reign over meaning and authenticity? Paragraph 124 of the *Constitution on the Sacred Liturgy* laid the groundwork for this concern by urging bishops to remove from churches works of art "that offend true religious sense . . . by the deficiency, mediocrity or sham in their artistic quality." Subsequent documents from Rome and the United States bishops have expanded on this.

In several places, the 2000 *General Instruction of the Roman Missal* speaks about the authenticity of liturgical signs. It reiterates, for example, the preference for communion under both kinds (#85 and 281) and for distributing elements consecrated at that Mass (#85). It notes that "the nature of the sign demands" that eucharistic bread look like food (#321) and that the Book of the Gospels and the lectionary serve "as signs and symbols of higher realities" and thus should be "worthy, dignified, and beautiful." (2000 GIRM, 349). We hear a warning in the 1978 statement, *Environment and Art in Catholic Worship,* from the U.S. Bishops' Committee on the Liturgy against minimalism in the liturgy: "Every word, gesture, movement, object, appointment must be real . . . not careless, phony, counterfeit, pretentious, exaggerated . . ."(#14). Quality and appropriateness, in particular, means being "capable of bearing the weight of mystery, awe, reverence and wonder which the liturgical action expresses" (#21). This criterion "rules out anything trivial and self-centered, anything fake, cheap or shoddy" (#22). Although this statement has been superceded by the 2000 guidelines, *Built of Living Stones* (BLS), its principles are still valid and the concern for quality and appropriateness is repeated (see BLS, 146–148).

These quotations provide the context in which paper purificators should be evaluated. Would their use be in the spirit of the documents just quoted? To me the obvious answer is no. Paper napkins are found in fast-food eateries rather than fine restaurants. They are associated with disposability rather than permanence. They convey the drive for what is easy, what needs no human attention in preparation or cleaning, what is adequate for the task, but needless of any larger world of human meaning and sensitivity. These are not the values upon which good liturgy is built.

Any argument used for paper purificators could probably also be used for paper or plastic chalices as well. Paper purificators may not offend sensitivities as much as plastic chalices would, but human sensitivity (or lack of it) is not the sole criterion for good liturgy. Other practices recently introduced need to be reevaluated in light of the quotations above. For example, what about electric votive "candles," reusable paschal candles (that is, the phony shell with the spring-loaded mini-candle inside), "lavabo" cloths and bowls that can fit in the palm of your hand, throw-away missalettes, artificial flowers?

Some may argue that a purificator is a minor item, that disposable purificators would be more sanitary, that high quality paper napkins look almost like cloth. But, as has been discussed often, communion from the cup poses no health problems from AIDS or any other communicable diseases (see also *The Communion Rite at Sunday Mass* by Gabe Huck, pp. 52–54, 58–59). Furthermore, if an object looks like something else, does that justify its use in the liturgy? Too many churches have "marble" altars which are really painted wood. Better to have a wood altar of quality than to have even a good imitation of marble!

The judgment of whether an item may be used for the liturgy should not depend on whether the item is "major" or "minor," or for that matter, costly or inexpensive. The liturgy is always an important activity, and everything used should be of a quality that reflects the beauty of God and the holy assembly gathered in prayer. Anything less is an affront to the assembly and to the sacredness of their activity.

Is it a good idea to applaud during the liturgy, for example, to show appreciation for the choir at the end of Mass, or as a sign of welcome to the newly baptized after the rite of baptism, or to congratulate the newlyweds after the rite of marriage? Why or why not?

One of the most moving moments for me during the funerals of Pope Paul VI and Pope John Paul I was when the coffins carrying the remains of these popes were taken from their place before Saint Peter's Basilica and brought into the church building for entombment. At both times, the assembly that had gathered together for prayer in Saint Peter's Square broke into muted yet heartfelt applause. Even at those moments of mourning, the human spirit felt it appropriate and necessary to express its admiration for these individuals in a public and audible manner, and so the assembly responded with spontaneous applause.

Psalm 47 begins with the words, "All you peoples, clap your hands! Shout to God with songs of joy!" Whether we allude to it or not, and whether it has been customary in some cultures and centuries or not, there is a religious tradition of expressing joy and emotion at prayer by clapping our hands and by loud shouts of joy. The pope often draws spontaneous applause from assemblies during his homilies or during the entrance or recessional processions when he presides at eucharist, especially on his many visits to various countries.

The Roman liturgical rites acknowledge that there are certain moments during the liturgy that call for an enthusiastic response from the assembly, a response often called an "acclamation" in the rubrics. Unfortunately, the standard acclamation of agreement, the single word "Amen," usually comes across as a mutter rather than a cheer, perhaps due to a cultural feeling that churches are not appropriate places to speak loudly. Yet it may be helpful to see where such moments for acclamations occur in existing liturgical rites to guide our reflections about the use of applause.

During the rites of ordination, at the formal "election" of a candidate for diaconal or presbyteral ordination (when the bishop says, "We choose these men, our brothers . . ."), the rite specifies that all present say, "Thanks be to God," or "give their assent to the choice in some other way." It is common for many assemblies to express this assent through applause. Similarly, in the rite of baptism, the rubrics note that after the sacramental bath (either pouring of water or immersion), "it is appropriate for the people to sing a short acclamation."

In the 1990 *Rite of Marriage* (not yet available in English), the words spoken by the presiding priest or deacon to receive the consent ("You have declared your consent . . ."), which now ends with a simple "Amen" by the assembly, will end with an acclamation of praise. A new rubric says, "The priest invites all present to praise God using the following or other acclamation. The priest says: Let us bless the Lord. The people answer: Thanks be to God."

These examples show that acclamations and assents are part of the revised Roman liturgical tradition, and that the rubrics permit alternatives to the simple "Thanks be to God."

When reflecting on the appropriateness of applause in liturgy, a distinction should be made between "celebration" and "performance." In our society, applause is usually associated with "a job well done." It is a response to a performance. But liturgy is never a performance by a few; it is a celebration by the whole. Applause can be quite appropriate as a ritual expression of assent or as a nonverbal, bodily acclamation within a liturgical action. Unfortunately, applause is often used to "thank" special people (musicians, liturgy planners, preachers), and this use of applause can subtly turn the celebrating assembly into a passive audience that expresses its approval of special performers as if those assembled were at a concert or play. This use of applause may warp the correct understanding of what the liturgical action is about. It would be better not to use applause in this manner.

But applause used as a liturgical response can be appropriate and even be recommended by the liturgical moment—as the examples cited in the rites of baptism, marriage and ordination suggest. If it seems appropriate to use applause as an alternative acclamation during a liturgical rite, it should be integrated into the rite (as usually happens during an ordination) rather than being tacked on in a disconnected way (as can frequently happen at weddings when the presider introduces "Mr. and Mrs. Bob and Mary Jones").

The church is still at a very early stage in introducing cultural adaptations into the liturgy. We still need to discern which elements from our culture are appropriate to liturgy, as well as the appropriate moments to use such new elements. Applause is one such cultural element. Any such discernment process will not be completed overnight, and sometimes openness to the Spirit and to liturgical tradition means that we may have to rethink established practices. If applause is used as an acclamation of joy at appropriate ritual moments, then its use could probably be continued without any problems. If applause is used in ways that reinforce the incorrect notion that liturgy is a performance, then such use should be scrutinized and perhaps discontinued, with careful explanation to the choir or whoever was recognized by the applause. The community should find other ways of congratulating and thanking such people.

Whatever is done, we always need to remember the basic nature of liturgy as a celebration of praise and thanks to God for Christ's death and resurrection, a celebration that involves all of who we are as human beings, both spirits and bodies!

What might we do about overcrowded Saturday evening Masses? Related to this weekly problem are the massive crowds who come to the Christmas Vigil and Midnight Masses. Do you have any thoughts?

The contemporary practice of Saturday vigil Masses is best understood by reflecting on the history of customs associated with the liturgical day. Somewhat arbitrarily, our contemporary secular society determines that a new day begins at midnight, but this is far from a universal custom in human history. Jewish custom still begins every new day with sunset, and such is the liturgical custom among some of the Eastern churches.

The Roman church makes use of two customs: For seasonal weekdays, memorials and feasts, the liturgical day coincides with the contemporary civil day and goes from midnight to midnight; but for Sundays and solemnities, the practice of beginning a new liturgical day with sunset of the previous evening is observed.

In earlier centuries, when social life was highly dependent upon natural light and activities after sunset were limited by the amount of fuel available for lamps and torches, the beginning of a new liturgical day, particularly on major feasts, was marked by evening prayer (vespers) around sunset (often including a lucernarium—the solemn lighting of a candle and praise of God for the gift of light). This liturgical rite commenced the new day's festivities and set the tone for personal prayer and reflection during that night prior to the celebration of the eucharist the next morning. In monasteries or smaller villages, there was never a question of Mass being celebrated other than in the morning of a feast day (except in the case of the Easter Vigil or Christmas Midnight Mass). We should also remember that, prior to the 1950s, the celebration of Mass at any time other than the morning was unknown.

Since about 1970 the church has permitted the faithful to satisfy the canonical obligation of attending Mass on Sundays and designated feasts at any time during the liturgical day, including the preceding evening. The rationale for such "anticipated" or vigil Masses is twofold. First, since the liturgical day on Sundays and major feasts begins with sunset, it makes sense not to distinguish between Masses celebrated at different times during the liturgical day. Second, since contemporary society is such that some people may not be free to participate in morning liturgies on Sundays or other festive days, the church has adapted its practices to the realities of contemporary society, primarily for the convenience of those unable to participate in the primary liturgical celebration. Nevertheless, it is one thing to allow a variety of practices, but it is something else to say that all practices are of equal value and stature.

With the exception of the Easter Vigil and the other liturgical celebrations of the Easter Triduum, the ideal of our liturgical tradition is that the primary gathering for liturgy should be on the day itself, and usually in the morning. The danger in ascribing to a Saturday vigil Mass the same status as that of a Sunday morning Mass is that people can easily reduce Sunday to the day on which they "have to go to Mass." Attending Saturday evening Mass means that Sunday itself can be left to other things. But Sunday is not merely the day on which the community gathers for the eucharist. Sunday is the weekly celebration of the Lord's resurrection, the day on which the community gathers to celebrate who it is as the body of Christ.

The church may now need to be countercultural and proclaim that Sundays should be kept holy by Christians refraining from work and praising God with other Christians. The apostolic letter *Dies Domini* of May 1998, on keeping holy the "Day of the Lord," is a beautiful meditation on the meaning of Sunday, many of the nuances of which are often overlooked. To begin to solve the dilemma proposed, perhaps the staff or pastoral council could begin by reading and studying this letter together.

Normally there should no more than one Saturday vigil Mass per parish, so if this celebration is always at or beyond capacity, perhaps the parish staff needs to consider articles in the parish bulletin addressing the importance of worship on Sunday itself. There may be other factors to consider, such as the schedule of Sunday morning Masses or the quality of music.

The primacy of the actual day of Sunday also applies to the primacy of any major feast, including Christmas. In some areas, it is becoming more and more popular to have multiple Masses on Christmas Eve at the expense of Masses on Christmas Day itself. Sometimes the vigil Mass is associated with childhood memories of Midnight Mass, at times with a desire to attend Mass early so that Christmas morning can be spent at home. Occasionally, a Christmas Eve Mass is planned as a children's Mass that attempts to give children a context for the exchange of presents, which, in some families, may occur after the liturgy on Christmas Eve. Once again, it is important to convey to the local community the priority of celebrating on the day itself. Although the motives for scheduling additional Christmas vigil Masses may be laudable, popular piety should be given proper direction by authentic liturgical tradition.

There is a proverb said to come from India that states the following: "There is more to life than increasing its speed." Closely associated with the rapid pace of contemporary Western culture is the high priority placed on convenience. The availability of vigil Masses may be a great blessing for those who must work on Sundays or parents who must attend Mass at different times because of a sick child at home. Yet it must also be acknowledged that, apart from the Easter Vigil, a vigil Mass should always be considered secondary to Masses on Sunday itself. Every Mass should be celebrated with the assistance of readers, eucharistic ministers, servers and music. Yet efforts should also be made to retain the priority of Sunday as the fundamental "Day of the Lord." Consequently, celebrations held on Sundays should always be given the utmost priority, not only in the manner in which they are celebrated, but also in the way that the parish community is encouraged to keep holy the "Day of the Lord."

May votive or ritual Mass texts be used on Sundays or solemnities?

The norms specifying when the Mass of the day may be replaced by another Mass are grounded in the *Constitution on the Sacred Liturgy*. It reiterates a truth often forgotten: Each Sunday the church celebrates the paschal mystery (#106). Thus other celebrations (of civil holidays or even saints) should not take precedence over Sundays or celebrations commemorating our salvation (#111). The basic principle is that the less important should not overwhelm the more important, nor should the specialized obscure the universal. These concerns were incorporated into the 2000 *General Instruction of the Roman Missal* and the *General Norms for the Liturgical Year and the Calendar* (GNLYC).

In the GIRM, there are four categories of liturgical days: The first category includes solemnities and their seasonal equivalents, such as the weekdays of Holy Week, Sundays of Advent, Lent and the Easter Season (see #372 for the complete list). On these days, even ritual Masses (for example, confirmation or nuptial Masses) and Masses for various needs and occasions are prohibited (#372, 374). Funeral Masses also are not allowed on most of these days (#380). The second category includes feasts, Sundays of Christmas and Ordinary Time, the last week of Advent, the Christmas octave and weekdays of Lent. On these days, ritual Masses may be used (subject to other norms) and, at the direction of the bishop, Masses for special needs. The third category includes obligatory memorials, the weekdays of Advent before December 17 and weekdays of the Easter Season after the Easter octave (see #376 for the complete list). On these days, the Mass of the day is to be celebrated, but for a real need alternate texts can be chosen. The fourth and final category includes optional memorials and weekdays in Ordinary Time. On these days, any Mass can be used, but ritual Masses are used only when the specific rite is to be celebrated (#355c, 377).

On Sundays in Ordinary Time, four sorts of changes can happen: (1) if a feast of the Lord or a solemnity falls on that date, it takes precedence over the Sunday; (2) certain ritual Masses with their own proper texts may be celebrated—the specific options can be found in each rite's introduction; (3) the Ordinary can decide that a Mass for a certain occasion is to be celebrated (for example, the bishop may decide that on "Mission Sunday," the Mass for the Spread of the Gospel are to be used); and (4) if a celebration having a "special appeal" to the community should occur on a weekday (for example, the patronal solemnity of the parish), it may be observed on Sunday if it would supersede the Sunday otherwise (GNLYC, 58–59).

When a conflict occurs, if a couple cannot be convinced to change their wedding date, two alternatives are possible. For some solemnities, it is possible to use the Mass of the day with the rite of marriage. Otherwise, celebrate the wedding outside of Mass. Outside of Mass, the wedding prayers and readings may always be used. At weddings celebrated on Sundays in Ordinary Time, the texts and readings for a nuptial Mass may be used provided the Mass is not a usually scheduled parish Mass.

What are good options for seating people who come late to Mass?

Over the years, punctuality for worship has been compromised by two attitudes. One is the traditional Catholic understanding that being late for Mass is tolerable as long as a person arrives before the reading of the gospel. The other is the cultural custom of being "fashionably late" for parties, dinners and similar social occasions.

When the Mass was celebrated in Latin without the active participation of all those present, seating latecomers was less of a distraction to those already present. Now, however, every detail needs to be arranged to enable and encourage the assembly to hear the word of God, respond in song and prayer, and be attentive. Distractions need to be prevented, especially during the proclamation of the readings and the homily.

There are several possible approaches to resolving this difficulty. One is catechesis. Bulletin announcements might explain that it is simple courtesy to arrive early for Mass in order to prepare for the communal act of worship. As baptized people, we engage in something of the utmost importance to ourselves and to the world when we worship God, and that responsibility requires that we be present and attentive when we begin the liturgy. Also, those who arrive early can help by filling up the seats from front to back, leaving those closest to the doors open for people running late. Ushers can assist in this.

A more drastic solution might involve holding latecomers near the door if they arrive during the opening prayer or one of the readings. It might work better in those churches that have a large vestibule from which latecomers can both see and hear the prayer or reading, and thus not be excluded. They might be seated during (or after) the psalm, or while all stand for the gospel acclamation. This solution requires well-trained ushers at every entrance—ministers capable of carrying out this task without being gruff or rude.

Another solution might be closing off the main aisle after the entrance procession, and allowing latecomers to take seats only via the side aisles. This would allow for the quick seating of latecomers without creating a major distraction.

Old habits are difficult to change. It will take a concerted effort to remind people that more is required at Mass than mere physical presence. While human distractions detract from divine worship, our assemblies nevertheless must welcome all who are sisters and brothers in Christ—even the tardy.

Our tabernacle is in a separate chapel, a good distance from the altar. Should we set up a temporary tabernacle in the sanctuary near the altar so that the communion ministers don't have to walk so far?

It is unfortunate that in many places, the tabernacle is still used for communion during Mass in much the same way it was before Vatican II. It is assumed by many priests and liturgy coordinators that someone always goes to the tabernacle for extra consecrated bread, that someone will return the excess to the tabernacle and that there is no real problem with this practice. But nowhere is the practice of distributing communion from the tabernacle during Mass explicitly permitted in any of the revised liturgical books.

The eucharist is reserved for the communion of the sick and the dying, and for worship outside of Mass. A careful reading of the *2000 General Instruction of the Roman Missal* leads one to conclude that the tabernacle is never approached during Mass except possibly to store excess consecrated hosts after communion (#163). Paragraphs 85 and 321 of the GIRM prescribe that enough bread and wine should be prepared for the communion of all present, and paragraph 49 of the *Ceremonial of Bishops* even directs that if a bishop must celebrate at an altar on which there is a tabernacle, the blessed sacrament should be removed (see 2000 GIRM, 315).

The presumption of the liturgical books is that enough elements are prepared for the communion of those present, but that there is not so much that it is impossible to consume what remains rather than reserve the excess in the tabernacle. This has been the traditional liturgical practice in churches who use the Byzantine rite, in which the excess eucharistic elements are carried to the side preparation table and always consumed, either by the deacon while the priest sings the solemn dismissal or by the priest himself after the dismissal. Consuming the excess consecrated elements is explicitly permitted by paragraph 13 of the 1980 document *Inaestimabile Donum* and by paragraph 163 of the 2000 GIRM. There is only one instance in the Roman tradition when it is explicitly mentioned that the excess consecrated bread is to be reserved in the tabernacle: on Holy Thursday for communion at the Good Friday liturgy.

The introduction to *Holy Communion and Worship of the Eucharist Outside of Mass* reminds us that "it is more in harmony with the nature of the celebration that, at the altar where Mass is celebrated, there should be no reservation of the sacrament in the tabernacle from the beginning of Mass" (#6). (See also 2000 GIRM, 315.) This is so because the celebration of Mass is a dynamic revelation of the eucharistic presence of Christ, whereas reservation of the blessed sacrament in a tabernacle is a static expression of the same presence. There is a subtle yet real clash of symbols when dynamic and static aspects of the same mystery compete with one another by being in close proximity.

With a bit of planning, it is possible to prepare an appropriate amount of bread and wine to consecrate for the communion of those present and have a minimal amount left over. An alert sacristan or liturgy coordinator might even be able to adjust discreetly the amount of bread and wine before the procession with the gifts.

Occasionally, one may run short of consecrated bread, even if the ministers divide some particles while distributing communion. The first option would be to obtain more eucharistic bread from one of the other ministers. Only when all the ministers need more should one person go to the tabernacle.

Once in a while the presence of very few communicants leads to an abundance of consecrated bread. In such a case, all the eucharistic bread should be gathered into one vessel at the altar. Then a single eucharistic minister can reverently carry the blessed sacrament to the tabernacle during the period of silence or a hymn of praise after communion.

Since the norm is that a church should have only one tabernacle, a second, "temporary" tabernacle in close proximity to the altar is inappropriate (#314).

The ideal of the GIRM — enough elements at each Mass for all communicants with no leftovers — is a worthy ideal. It takes careful planning, but it is not unattainable.

What is the significance of the various colors for vesture? Is blue an official liturgical color for Advent? Does the altar cloth have to be the same color as the chasuble?

Before the twelfth century there were no universal rules specifying which color vestments should be worn on which liturgical days. There seemed to be only a general rule, one still followed in some Eastern churches, that joyous feasts assume brighter colors and that penitential and somber occasions assume darker colors. At the beginning of the twelfth century, the Augustinian Canons at Jerusalem prescribed a scheme which was then modified, simplified and incorporated into the Roman Missal of 1570. The twelfth-century scheme proposed associations that we might consider odd today, such as the use of black on Christmas and on the feasts of Mary, and the use of blue on Epiphany and on Ascension.

The *General Instruction of the Roman Missal* does not mention the significance or symbolism of the various colors when it specifies their usage (#346). But a common interpretation of the major colors is this: White is reminiscent of purity, joy, life and light (and thus is used during the Christmas and Easter seasons, on feasts of Christ, Mary and saints who were not martyrs, and at baptisms, weddings and, in the United States, funerals). Red is associated with fire and blood (and thus is used on Pentecost and at other Masses of the Holy Spirit, on feasts associated with Christ's Passion, for martyrs, and for confirmation). Green reminds people of growth, latent life and hope (and is used in Ordinary Time). Violet is associated with penance, sadness and royalty (and is used in Advent and Lent, and for funerals).

Two other colors may be used at choice: black (associated with mourning) for Masses of the Dead and rose (a lighter shade of violet) marking the midpoints of Advent (on the Third Sunday) and Lent (on the Fourth Sunday).

In the Roman church, blue was never a universally used liturgical color, although in the nineteenth century it was permitted by indult in Spain and in Spanish missionary territories (such as Mexico and California) for the feast of the Immaculate Conception. Associating blue with Mary is relatively recent, since the oldest Eastern icons usually depict the Mother of God with a dark red or maroon mantle. In certain cities that followed ancient liturgical traditions, other colors were prescribed. For example, Lyons, France, uses ashen gray for most of Lent.

The 1978 *Lutheran Book of Worship* was one of the first modern liturgical books to prescribe the use of blue for the season of Advent, citing precedence in Sweden and in the Mozarabic rite of Toledo, Spain.

At present, therefore, the liturgical color for Advent remains violet. Yet various authors have rightly pointed out that vestments used in Lent, the penitential period prior to the Easter Triduum, may not always be appropriate in Advent, the preparation period prior to Christmas. A number of authors suggest using different sets of vestments in different shades of purple for Advent and for Lent. For example, some have suggested the use of darker purples in Advent, approximating the darkness of night or the deep purple hues of landscape after sunset, and the use of redder violets in Lent, hinting of the red of Passion Sunday and Good Friday.

The color of vestments is one way to mark the change of the liturgical season as well as its mood. The liturgical color of vestments might also be used in other ways in the worship space. At one time, the Roman Missal prescribed that altars be completely covered with a cloth (the antependium or frontal) of the liturgical color of the day. Over this cloth were to be placed the three white altar cloths. It also was prescribed that the tabernacle veil match the color of the day as well.

Such details are no longer prescribed by the liturgical books, but the underlying principle is still valid. Different colors do affect us differently. Using the color of the season or feast for more than the vestments of the priest can help mark the tone and the atmosphere for prayer.

If you enjoyed the answers to these questions, look for *Q&A: Seasons, Sacraments and Sacramentals* by Dennis C. Smolarski, SJ. Available from Liturgy Training Publications, it is a book of frequently asked questions and insightful answers about celebrating the other sacraments and sacramentals. Visit our website at www.ltp.org, send a message to orders@ltp.org or call 1-800-933-1800.

And receive a regular dose of Dennis Smolarski's pastoral wisdom by reading his Q&A column in *Rite* magazine, published eight times a year (January, February/March, April, May/June, July, August/September, October and November/December). To subscribe, visit our website at www.ltp.org, send a message to orders@ltp.org or call 1-800-933-4213. The magazine also gives you an invitation and e-mail address by which you can submit *your* questions about any aspect of liturgy. Individual, group and foreign rates are available.